# 12 Steps for the
# RECOVERING
# PHARISEE
## (like me)

Jack —

In appreciation for your
fine work.

*John Fischer*

# Books by John Fischer

FROM BETHANY HOUSE PUBLISHERS

*Ashes on the Wind*

*Saint Ben*

*The Saints' and Angels' Song*

*True Believers ~~Don't~~ Ask Why*

*12 Steps for the Recovering Pharisee (like me)*

# 12 Steps for the RECOVERING PHARISEE

## (like me)

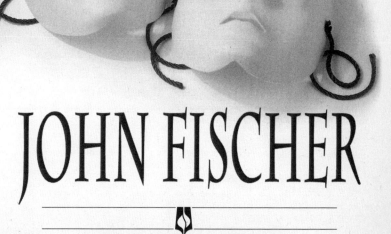

# JOHN FISCHER

BETHANY HOUSE PUBLISHERS
MINNEAPOLIS, MINNESOTA 55438

Published by Bethany House Publishers
A Ministry of Bethany Fellowship International
11400 Hampshire Avenue South
Minneapolis, Minnesota 55438
www.bethanyhouse.com

Printed in the United States of America by
Bethany Press International, Minneapolis, Minnesota 55438

**Library of Congress Cataloging-in-Publication Data**

Fischer, John, 1947–
   12 steps for the recovering Pharisee (like me) / by John Fischer.
      p.   cm.
   ISBN 0–7642–2202–3 (pbk.)
      1. Christian life.  2. Pharisees—Miscellanea.  I. Title: Twelve steps for
the recovering Pharisee (like me).  II. Title.
BV4509.5   .F45      2000
248.4—dc21                                                                99–050590

My courage to speak in this book has been bolstered by certain Christian writers and speakers who have chosen to tell the truth about themselves and their humanity, giving little regard to their reputations. These people make no secret of their sins and struggles, leaving us with a true picture of God's grace and no confusion as to who they, and consequently we, are to follow. Though there are others, the ones who have had a most profound effect on my life of faith would be Frederick Buechner, C. S. Lewis, Brennan Manning, and my pastor, Chuck Smith Jr. I would like to acknowledge them for their courage. I would also like to thank Christopher Soderstrom for his editing and for the excellent study questions at the conclusion of this book.

JOHN FISCHER, pioneering musician, songwriter, and popular speaker, is also the award-winning author of many books. For years his insightful columns have been a favorite monthly feature in *Contemporary Christian Music Magazine*. A graduate of Wheaton College, John and his family now live in California.

# Contents

# Introduction

As I have grown to understand the gospel and learn more of God's grace, I have also become conscious of a corresponding struggle with pride and self-righteousness. Like anyone, I want to be well thought of. I am often conscious, as I am even now, of picking my words carefully, like walking through a minefield of impressions, so as to appear honest while stopping short of the naked truth that might implicate me more than I am willing. It is a problem that the Pharisees of Jesus' day sought to overcome by concealing themselves behind a whitewashed religious veneer.

So when a gentleman came up to me at a summer music festival at which I was teaching and commented on how he had found my writings to be, for him, like a twelve-step plan for recovering Pharisees, I realized that I had been working on rooting out this problem for quite a while, though until now it had never been the focus of my work. I decided it was time to make it such. His fingering of this correlation struck a chord in me, as did the use of the recovery model as a creative approach to this chronic spiritual disease.

My use of the recovery model in this book admittedly is somewhat tongue-in-cheek. I am not expecting Pharisee recovery groups to spring up all over the country as a result of my discussions here (though it might not be such a bad idea), nor am I expecting people to see these steps as some sort of methodology through which they can accomplish the permanent eradication of pride and self-projected superiority. I am more interested in borrowing the recovery model as a way of unmasking, and potentially freeing us from, the intoxication of spiritual pride and prejudice that continually lures believers away from the grace, gratitude, and life of astonishment that the Spirit of God desires for us.

It is my firm belief that the prideful attitude of the Pharisees and the practice of measuring out righteousness are problems that affect not only Christians but everyone at some point. They are built into human nature. They even accompany other religions and cults. Pharisaism always seems to show up whenever righteousness is pursued in any form, at any level. Acceptance on the basis of performance was how most of us began our lives, and it's not easy to shake. In biblical history this is called the Old Covenant.

The Old Covenant requires a standard of performance and a reason to be obedient to it. But the standard, in its truest form, is impossible to pull off consistently. It could be argued that this is the whole point of God's dealings with humanity through the covenants. The Old Covenant is there to break us, to show us that we cannot live according to its precepts—that sin and selfishness dwell in us to a significant degree so as to rule out the possibility of following even the clear call of Jesus to love God, self, and others. This inability to follow the standard, along with its accompanying humility, qualifies us for a Savior—someone who will fulfill the law on our behalf and grant us righteousness as a free gift. This is God's grace as given to us in the New Covenant through the death and resurrection of our Lord and Savior Jesus Christ.

The Pharisees enter the picture as the ones who figure out a way to make the Old Covenant work for them, thus making the new one unnecessary. As official interpreters of the laws of God, they adapt the standard through their own interpretation until the law (actually, their version of it) becomes something that is not impossible to perform but indeed quite possible, though difficult and meticulous at times. The "standard" is set so that attaining it is difficult enough to weed out the undesirables but not so difficult as to become overly burdensome—and that's the key. Armed with this new standard, Pharisees can then qualify themselves for righteousness and judge those who, according to their measurement, fall short. Once this course is entered upon, it can branch into myriad avenues of arrogance, judgment, and false humility.

What makes pharisaical sin so dangerous is that it disguises itself as a form of enlightenment. This is what Jesus meant when he said, "If then the light within you is darkness, how great is that darkness!" (Matthew 6:23).

The darkness is great because one is deluded into thinking it is light. You think you are seeing better than anyone else, when, in fact, you can't see at all. This means the idea that you can't see is farthest from you. A blind person *knows* he is blind. A Pharisee *thinks* he can see, and this is why the "light" within him is actually darkness. Jesus called the Pharisees "blind guides."

So it is necessary in this darkness that we call light to identify our error and get free from our entrapment—exactly the job of all recovery groups. It could even be argued that our churches ought to be more like this. The church should be the most honest place on earth—a place where it is possible to say among friends: "Hi, I'm John, and I'm a Pharisee."

"Hi, John," comes the echo, and we revel in the realization that this is the meeting place of accountability for equals. These are the Simons who want to come down off their pedestals and join the company of saved sinners at the feet of Jesus, who, like the prostitute anointing his feet with perfume and tears, can't seem to get enough of this grace and forgiveness. This is the gospel for those courageous enough to tear off their masks of adequacy and self-righteousness and get on with a life of gratitude and love for others. This is the Pharisee recovery group of which I speak, and these are the steps that will lead us out. I know, for I am an expert in the downturned look, the haughty eye, the wagging head—and I've had enough of it.

Welcome to the group.

**Step 1** We admit that our single most unmitigated pleasure is to judge other people.

**Step 2** Have come to believe that our means of obtaining greatness is to make everyone lower than ourselves in our own mind.

**Step 3** Realize that we detest mercy being given to those who, unlike us, haven't worked for it and don't deserve it.

**Step 4** Have decided that we don't want to get what we deserve after all, and we don't want anyone else to either.

**Step 5** Will cease all attempts to apply teaching and rebuke to anyone but ourselves.

**Step 6** Are ready to have God remove all these defects of attitude and character.

**Step 7** Embrace the belief that we are, and will always be, experts at sinning.

**Step 8** Are looking closely at the lives of famous men and women of the Bible who turned out to be ordinary sinners like us.

**Step 9** Are seeking through prayer and meditation to make a conscious effort to consider others better than ourselves.

**Step 10** Embrace the state of astonishment as a permanent and glorious reality.

**Step 11** Choose to rid ourselves of any attitude that is not bathed in gratitude.

**Step 12** Having had a spiritual awakening as the result of these steps, we will try to carry this message to others who think that Christians are better than everyone else.

STEP

# 1

*We admit that
our single most
unmitigated pleasure
is to judge
other people.*

*I've been in my mind;*
*It's such a fine line*
*That keeps me searchin'*
*for a heart of gold.*

NEIL YOUNG

---

FEW ACTIVITIES IN LIFE RIVAL THE THRILL OF PASSING JUDGMENT on another human being. I don't believe I can go a day on God's green earth without in some way indulging in this forbidden art. It is the particular pastime of the self-righteous to hold court, and I have been long at the bar. For me, judgment and condemnation have become a way of life. The act of mental sentencing is the mind-set most readily available to those who are neither willing nor prepared to bring their own actions, thoughts, and motivations into the light.

In a small part of an average day, I might condemn my daughter numerous times for a messy room; my son, for laziness; my wife, for working too hard (and raising my standard); even my dog, for his bad odor. (Of course I am responsible for his bad odor because I haven't given him a bath—he's just a dog.) I pick up the newspaper in the morning (after condemning the paperboy for throwing it so that half the front page is torn) and find it full of people I can judge as being sinful, ignorant, stupid, arrogant, or childish. Lumping large groups of people together and at once dispatching the whole lot of them is especially effective. The world always seems to cooperate with my assessment of it as long as I remain distant from a personal knowledge of any of these individuals.

I get in my car and start driving and find a host of inept vehicle

14

operators who all should have failed their driving tests. I arrive miraculously unscathed at my bank and find myself in line behind another group of people who obviously can't add or subtract, or they wouldn't take so long at the counter. At the market, I complain to myself about the lack of organization that renders it impossible to find what I'm looking for, about the inane Muzak coming from the speakers, about the new labeling process that makes it difficult to price individual items, about the ads that interrupt the Muzak telling me about the specials of the day up the aisles I've already passed, and about the teenage checker who is just a little too loopy and bouncy for my current mood.

"Paper or plastic?" she smiles, working a too-large wad of gum around in her too-small open mouth.

Ever notice how everything that is wrong with the world is always someone else's fault? We like it this way.

Our eyes look out, they do not look in, and if they are looking for what is wrong, they will always find much upon which to focus. Only inner eyes can look in, and inner eyes do not come naturally. Inner eyes are weak, at best, and rarely exercised. It is our "out-look" that predominates—an outlook that takes great pleasure in scrutinizing the minutest detail of someone else's compromise while overlooking large chunks of our own self-contradiction with nary a blink.

This is not hard to understand when we consider the fact that our minds exist to ourselves alone. My thoughts are my thoughts. I sit in judgment because I am housed in my own judge's chamber. I think to myself, rationalize by myself, decide for myself. I am the author and finisher of my own perspective. I see it my way, and my way is most certainly going to be judged by myself as being right. Given this, why would I ever place myself on the witness stand in my own mind? Why be questioned when I can be the judge?

This is perhaps the gravest misuse of our God-given privilege of possessing a mind: secrecy and autonomy. A mind does not have to tell. It does not have to bend to any other authority—any other perspective—than its own. It can even feign compliance while all along it continues to judge. I can sit in my own chair, with my own righteous robes pulled tightly around me, and no one will know.

This is one of the reasons why we like judging so much; we can hold court in the privacy of our own mind and there is no one to disagree with us. So long as we remain our own authority, we do not have to be challenged. We can carry on with our own conclusions about ourselves and others, even if they contradict reality, because we are in charge of all the conclusions, and we can bolster our story however we want.

Sometimes we listen to our own lies so much that we begin to sincerely believe them. This is precisely why Jesus had his greatest argument with those among the Pharisees whose view of reality did not jive with the way things really are. The "light" they carried around was a false view of reality that distorted all their judgments (see the Introduction).

This is why a recovery model is appropriate for Pharisees who don't want to be Pharisees anymore. Recovery assumes a behavioral pattern that is beyond the ability of a person to identify or control. The lies are too strong, the justifications and rationalizations are too convincing, the denials are too dense, and the inner eyes are too weak to overcome without—as in all recovery programs—some outside help from those who are going through similar struggles and are perhaps a bit further down the road. It's going to take help from outside ourselves to get at this nasty problem, and even then, like any addiction, the possibility of relapse will always be present.

## Why do we like judging so much?

The act of judging gives us a subjective means of affirming ourselves. No matter what I've done or how bad I am, I can always comfort myself by finding someone out there who is "worse" than I am. I can also bring down those who appear to be more worthy than me by finding or manufacturing some flaw in their character that allows me to be better than they are in my mind. This is the means by which we establish a pharisaical sense of self-worth. If I can show that I am better than someone else—anyone else—then I can think of myself as being worthy based on that assessment alone. I can place a value on myself that can be confirmed by repeatedly finding someone further down the moral ladder, or something afoul with those further up.

This is why, whether we're aware of it or not, we're secretly glad when spiritual leaders fall into sin: Someone who we thought was doing better than we are is, in fact, no better than us. Oh, what glee! Even though we have not improved upon ourselves in any significant way, we *feel* better because the "standard" has been altered to accommodate our own shortcomings. We are now equal to, if not above, the holy man, and for a while, for all the wrong reasons, it feels good.

Jesus caught the Pharisees at this trick, even read into their private prayers what was really going on in their minds. He knew the condition of their hearts, and his Father had heard plenty of these prayers, if indeed any of them ever made it to his place in heaven. One gospel account has a Pharisee praying *to himself*, which would have made the prayer irrelevant whether God ever heard anything or not. It wasn't for God that he was praying; it was for his own benefit. "God, I thank you that I am not like other men—robbers, evildoers, adulterers . . ." (Luke 18:11–12). *I am not like other men. I am different; I am better.* It is the creed of the Pharisee to be better than everyone else and to devise means of measuring and comparing that support this assessment. *I fast twice a week and give a tenth of all I get.* Thus the Pharisee establishes an attainable standard that becomes both a measure of personal righteousness and a yardstick for judging others. Certainly the robbers and evildoers and adulterers this Pharisee was referring to were not fasting or giving a tenth.

That's because the robbers and evildoers and adulterers have no clue this game is even going on. They don't care. They don't associate with the Pharisee any more than he does with them. Most likely they are completely oblivious to the idea of fasting and tithing, and yet they have been judged by their apparent disregard for both in the Pharisee's mind.

This is one of the great pleasures of passing judgment. It isn't a requirement to explain either the rules or the judgment to anyone; the fact is, one may raise and lower the bar at will. The purpose of this judgment is not the real betterment of anyone, nor is it to find the truth—to know what the real standard of judgment is and to put oneself under its scrutiny. Its purpose is only to establish a self-defined superiority over others.

We call the shots. We make the rules. We draw the line in the sand and then step over it, leaving everyone else on the other side. It's a fool-proof way to feel good about ourselves.

## It's all about control

"Woe to you, teachers of the law and Pharisees, you hypocrites! You shut the kingdom of heaven in men's faces. You yourselves do not enter, nor will you let those enter who are trying to" (Matthew 23:13).

Such a sad state. Why don't they enter? Because entering might mean losing control. It might mean being overwhelmed with unspeakable joy and gratitude. It might turn them embarrassingly giddy with generosity. Can't let that happen! Above all, it might mean losing control over who gets in and who doesn't. Imagine having to exist forever in the kingdom of heaven with people you detest! For the Pharisee, being the gatekeeper—and therefore controlling who gets in and who stays out—is more desirable than enjoying the fruits of entering in.

Notice how obvious it is to Jesus that these Pharisees and representatives of the law have not entered the kingdom of heaven. Had they entered, they would not be judging—there would be no reason to judge, since heaven is made up of people who arrive there on no merit of their own. In the kingdom of heaven, they would have been indulging in all the benefits of heaven. They would have immediately recognized Jesus as coming from God, since they claimed to know God so well, and they would have invited all to come and enjoy what they had found. They would have been basking in a sense of worthiness that comes from God's love and acceptance of them, and not through any manipulation of their own. As it was, they became self-appointed gatekeepers, holding the keys to something they never experienced and making sure that, if they couldn't have it, at least no one else would either.

This sounds all too familiar.

It's the Pharisee in us that wants control, and more than anything we want control over the rules of the game. (This is common to all religions.) When we follow this pattern, it works to our supposed advantage in the following way: We set a standard that some, but not all, are capable of achieving. This standard usually has the weight of an acceptable authority behind it (in the Pharisees' case it was the law of Moses; with today's Christians it can be one's interpretation of the Bible), and yet it is conveniently reinterpreted and reduced to some nitpicky list of do's and don'ts that some people can't do and others simply don't care about, with good reason.

For the original Pharisees this amounted to things like washing hands before eating, observing the Sabbath by not lifting a finger, fasting twice a week, and giving a tenth of all they had to the temple. Each one of these was done with great display since, as Jesus pointed out, everything the Pharisees did was for show (Matthew 23:5).

For today's Pharisee, certain cultural taboos serve the same purpose, such as smoking, drinking, dancing, and attending R-rated movies, for instance. Abstaining from these things appears sacrificial, but most modern-day Pharisees don't want to do any of these things anyway. This system cleverly enables us to follow the law perfectly (as we have reinterpreted it) while passing judgment on all those who don't follow it, can't follow it, or who simply couldn't care less about our little charade.

And behind this penchant to trivialize holiness by sacrificing what is really no great sacrifice can be hidden many deeper, more important matters of the heart. Jesus said, "You have a fine way of setting aside the commands of God in order to observe your own traditions!" (Mark 7:9). And what are these commands? "The more important matters of the law—justice, mercy and faithfulness" (Matthew 23:23).

## Justice, mercy, and faithfulness

If they would have gone after the more important matters that Jesus suggested, all the silly little games of the Pharisees would have ceased to exist.

For instance, the pursuit of justice would have forced them to admit their own guilt, for Jesus redefined lawlessness in such a way as to leave no one righteous—not one. Six times in the Sermon on the Mount he says, "You have heard that it was said . . ." and six times he follows with "but I tell you . . ." Each time what the Pharisees heard was a familiar definition of a law redefined by Jesus as to its formidable *essence*. In each case the Pharisee version is doable, while the Jesus version is not. "Do not murder" becomes "do not become angry with anyone." "Do not commit adultery" becomes "do not look upon a woman lustfully." "Divorce only with a certificate" becomes "divorce equals adultery." "Do not break your oath" becomes "do not swear at all." And "return an eye for an eye and a tooth for a tooth" becomes "do not resist an evil person, but return good for evil." With justice thus redefined, who can escape condemnation? No one.

Jesus caught the Pharisees at the heart of their evil scheme just as he catches us at the heart of ours. There's a delicate balance here. The pharisaical goal is to make the commands of righteousness just easy enough for me to follow, but too difficult (or irrelevant) for almost everyone else. That will allow me to look pretty good while leaving me plenty of people to judge.

Too bad the Pharisees couldn't have seen that Jesus was also giving them a chance to know something wonderful—the mercy of God. Only when justice has forced someone to realize their guilt can the mercy of God come into play. God sets us up for his kindness by hitting us hard with his impartiality. We are all guilty; we can all have mercy. Or as Paul states it, "The law was added so that the trespass might increase. But where sin increased, grace increased all the more" (Romans 5:20).

Yet here's the rub: even after hearing about God's mercy, I still err by choosing mercy for me and justice for everyone else. I like the idea of God having mercy on me because I am an exceptionally nice guy. I deserve mercy. But all those scoundrels out there who cheat on their wives . . . no way! It's justice for them!

I can't have it both ways.

This is actually pretty easy to understand, and it brings clarity to other warnings of Jesus about casting judgment. If anyone else gets justice, I must get justice too. On the other hand, if I get mercy, everyone else gets mercy; I can't be partial to myself in either case. And this is where the Pharisees went astray. They were partial, and in their partiality, they condemned themselves before God.

It's clear to see why Jesus doesn't want us to judge others: We don't stand a chance. If I judge even one person, I announce that judgment is the basis upon which I want everyone evaluated—myself included (Matthew 7:1). This is the law of impartiality. You want to judge? Fine, get ready to face the Judge.

In the same way, if I want mercy for me, then I have to allow it for everyone else, even those who, in my estimation, are "worse" sinners than I. This is the big picture that we all need to see: Justice for all; condemnation for all. A cross and an empty tomb for all; mercy for all.

This leaves us with faithfulness—the one ongoing quality God asks of us. He is willing to justify us; he is willing to grant us mercy instead of the condemnation we deserve, but he does ask for a life of faithfulness.

Faithfulness here is in contrast to perfection. Being faithful is a far cry from being perfect. Faithfulness means being authentic, devoted, consistent, loyal. An alcoholic who regularly shows up at A.A. meetings is faithful. She may slip and fall, but she is faithful to get up again. She may lie to her supervisor, but she is faithful to tell the truth when confronted. Faithfulness allows for failure; perfection does not.

When God calls for perfection, it is assumed that I cannot perform it. It's the demand for perfection that keeps me relying on God's mercy and grace. But the call to faithfulness is a call I can answer. Faithful to follow, faithful to confess, faithful to obey, faithful to repent, faithful to believe, faithful to pray and seek God—all these are the requirements of faithfulness. All of them are doable and are, in fact, my responsibility and my joy, having been the unexpected recipient of so great a mercy.

The Pharisees could have had it all if they would have been willing to admit their hypocrisy and join the rest of the human race on their knees before a merciful Lord. "God, have mercy on me, a sinner," cried the publican in the parable of Jesus (Luke 18:13). Imagine, if you will, a Pharisee in his long robe, his phylacteries, and his ornate turban, down on his knees next to the tax collector in tears of repentance and joy. Imagine these two embracing, both overwhelmed at the mercy of God in hearing and answering the same prayer. There you have a true picture of the kingdom of God. It's hard to imagine the Pharisee standing up after such an experience and judging anyone.

Remember the words of Jesus:

> Be merciful, just as your Father is merciful. Do not judge, and you will not be judged. Do not condemn, and you will not be condemned. Forgive, and you will be forgiven. Give and it will be given to you. A good measure, pressed down, shaken together and running over, will be poured into your lap. For with the measure you use, it will be measured to you. (Luke 6:36–38)

What an incredible proposition. Want love? Give love. Want mercy? Give mercy. Want acceptance? Give acceptance. Want to judge? Get ready to be judged. Want to escape judgment? Don't judge at all. Don't do it. Get with those who want to get over this problem and remind each other of God's grace.

*Step 1* We admit that our single most unmitigated pleasure is to judge other people.

*Step 2* Have come to believe that our means of obtaining greatness is to make everyone lower than ourselves in our own mind.

*Step 3* Realize that we detest mercy being given to those who, unlike us, haven't worked for it and don't deserve it.

*Step 4* Have decided that we don't want to get what we deserve after all, and we don't want anyone else to either.

*Step 5* Will cease all attempts to apply teaching and rebuke to anyone but ourselves.

*Step 6* Are ready to have God remove all these defects of attitude and character.

*Step 7* Embrace the belief that we are, and will always be, experts at sinning.

*Step 8* Are looking closely at the lives of famous men and  women of the Bible who turned out to be ordinary sinners like us.

*Step 9* Are seeking through prayer and meditation to make a conscious effort to consider others better than ourselves.

*Step 10* Embrace the state of astonishment as a permanent and glorious reality.

*Step 11* Choose to rid ourselves of any attitude that is not bathed in gratitude.

*Step 12* Having had a spiritual awakening as the result of these steps, we will try to carry this message to others who think that Christians are better than everyone else.

STEP

# 2

*We have come to believe*

*that our means of obtaining*

*greatness is to make everyone*

*lower than ourselves*

*in our own mind.*

( Everyone feels morally superior
to someone.

J O H N   I R V I N G )

---

**M**Y WIFE NEEDED FAX PAPER FOR AN ANTICIPATED BUSY DAY IN her home office, so I took a break from this writing to pay an early morning visit to an office supply store. As typically happens, there were other supplies I needed once I got there and saw them on the shelves, so by the time I made it to the lone checkout stand I had an armful. After waiting a few minutes for the customer in front of me (who looked like he was supplying the Pentagon with new office equipment), a clerk across the way announced, "I'll help the next in line over here." The lady immediately behind me, with two items in her hand, made a beeline for the open counter and never looked back. So I followed her over, "next in line" again, but comforted by the prospect of a shorter wait.

While I stood there, staring at the back of the head of the woman who used to be behind me, I began to notice things I didn't like about her hair. It was cropped abruptly in the back and the color job was fading. *Probably did it herself,* I thought. Then, in my mind, I put words in her mouth: *"I'm sorry, but I've only got a couple things here—do you mind if I jump in front of you?"* Something like that would have been nice. *"Of course not,"* I would have been happy to say, *"go right ahead."* At the least it would have been courteous to acknowledge my presence and my rightful place in front of her. Then I wondered where she bought such

26

dowdy clothes. And just when I was about to explore some disparaging thoughts on the subject of her rather wide rear end, made even more prominent by a poor choice of sweat pants, I remembered that I was writing about the human propensity to put others below us.

As I drove home humbled and slightly humiliated by becoming, so quickly, a graphic illustration of my own point, I wondered about other ways I could have handled this situation, even if only in my mind. First, I recalled an incident when I did a similar thing to someone else. I cut in front of a guy in line once, and he made it clear to me and everyone else in the store, in no uncertain terms, exactly what I had done. I had not intentionally cut in front of the man; I simply had been so engrossed in my own thoughts that I didn't pay attention to where the end of the line actually was. Perhaps the same thing happened to this woman. Maybe she didn't intentionally ignore me; maybe she was just *unaware* of me. Having identified the same behavior in myself, I could now forgive her more easily and avert the judgment, as well as forgive myself for the judgmental thoughts I had toward her.

Second, I began to realize that if I could sit down and talk face-to-face with her, I would no doubt find that there was a real live person there. I'd made a prejudgment of her that had nothing to do with her real self. She might be a Christian. She might be a social worker. She might have a tremendous sense of humor. She might be a criminal judge or a criminal. She was probably somebody's mother, somebody's sister, somebody's wife, and if none of these, she was at least somebody's child. She loved and was loved by someone (by God, to be certain), she hoped and dreamed, and like all of us she has an eternal destiny.

These two reflections form the bulk of my thoughts for this second step in overcoming pharisaical judgments: (1) Put yourself in the place of the person you are tending to judge, and (2) give them the benefit of the doubt.

No matter where we find ourselves on the social ladder, we can always find someone below us. It's human nature. When I was little and I thought my parents were being unreasonable to me, I would take it out on my dog. I watch the same thing happen with my kids. Our poor pets sometimes bear the brunt of being lowest on the totem pole.

This is also the kind of thinking that, fueled by group superiority, can foster prejudice and racial bigotry and lead ultimately to "ethnic cleansing" and holocaust. These attitudes continually repeat themselves in history: the Germans and the Jews, the Catholics and the Protestants, the Hutus and the Tutsis, the Serbs and the Albanians, the Ku Klux Klan and the African-Americans, the Turks and the Kurds . . . and there appears to be no letup. The shortest route to ascendancy is the degradation of someone or some group. It is a dangerous and deadly shortcut to self-esteem that never arrives at its destination.

How can this tendency be avoided? In the same manner I thought my way out of judging the woman who jumped in front of me in the office supply store—by first putting myself in her shoes, and then by giving her the benefit of the doubt.

## Stand awhile in someone else's shoes

Bob Dylan, master of put-downs, once lamented that he wished a certain individual could stand inside his shoes and discover what a drag they were from his perspective. This sounds like a judgment in its own right, but in typical Dylan style it turns one's judgment in on one's self. It can be seen as a last-ditch effort to help this person see his inconsistencies and mend his ways.

Jesus made much of a similar blindness of the Pharisees: They imagined they were seeing when actually they were blind. His words to them were every bit as caustic as Dylan's words.

Once, after healing a blind man, Jesus said to the Pharisees who were watching, "For judgment I have come into this world, so that the blind will see and those who see will become blind."

To which the Pharisees replied, "What? Are we blind too?"

He said, "If you were blind, you would not be guilty of sin; but now that you claim you can see, your guilt remains" (John 9:39–41).

If the Pharisees could have seen themselves as Jesus saw them—as blind guides and fools—then they could have come to Christ and been given sight. As it was, they refused to accept their blindness, claimed they could see just fine—just as well as Jesus, for that matter—and never saw themselves for who they really were. Jesus was the Bob Dylan in their lives. *If you guys could see yourselves as I see you, you'd know how foolish you look.*

We need to learn to see ourselves through other people's eyes to see ourselves as we really are.

My kids have often played this role in my life. When they were younger, they would exasperate me by laughing at me when I got mad at them for misbehaving or not listening. Of course, the little smirks on their faces would only increase my ire. I simply could not get any respect. And when I lost all hope and went to my wife for support, she would get a similar smile on her face—as if they were in on this together!

"You really should see yourself," she would say later (for my own benefit), trying to be loving but still delivering the sad facts. "The veins in your forehead pop out and your face gets real red. It's like something in a *MAD Magazine* cartoon. Good heavens, you're scaring them, John. It's good they can laugh instead of thinking you're turning into some kind of monster, because that's what you look like when you act this way. They can't help it. It's so out of character for you that all they can do is laugh."

Now, I'm not sure that news fully resolved the respect issue, but it did serve to force me to see another perspective on myself. We all need people around us with enough courage and love to tell us the truth about ourselves. How do other people see us? We're so self-centered that it's hard to know. We need to be open to someone else's perspective and, in some cases, to ask for it.

I'm sure we all know someone who combs ten inches of hair (count the strands) over a wide, shiny bald dome and actually thinks he is concealing something. This hopeless cover-up is similar to whatever we think we are hiding that in reality everyone sees. The problem is, most people, out of common courtesy or more likely fear of embarrassment, don't tell us what they see. Like talking to someone with bad breath or food on their face, they let us go on to offend or amuse some other unsuspecting soul. The first thing about standing in someone else's shoes is that you see yourself for the first time without all your blind spots and cover-ups.

Think about it this way: If I'm judging the lady in front of me, there's a good chance someone behind me is doing the same thing to me. And if they are, what do they see? That's what Bob Dylan wanted us to think about. He wanted someone to know what they really looked like to someone else, not what they thought they looked like. Our version of ourselves is always different than that of others. It's the difference between seeing yourself in a regular mirror—the straight-on reflection we always get—and seeing yourself in a three-way mirror, where you suddenly see angles on yourself you've never seen before. It's shocking when this first happens, almost like someone else is in the room.

For me, that multiple-mirror view is a disaster because it shows me a very wide bald spot on the back of my head that I normally never have to see. I usually see, instead, from the front-view mirror, a light density of fine hair on the top of my head that looks like more than it really is because I'm looking *through it*, not *down on it*. This wasteland for hair I harbor on the back side of my head is visible only to the guy behind me in line. So what's he thinking? He sees the truth. He sees in front of him what I seldom see: a bald guy.

It's virtually impossible to get another view of yourself by yourself. Just like we need at least two mirrors to see the angles most other people see of us, we need other people to tell us who we really are. People can serve as our character mirrors, and we need to be vulnerable to what they tell us. My wife and children think I look silly when I get mad. My anger obviously is not having the effect on them that I envision. I think they should be cowering, and they are laughing. I interpret their laughter as disrespect, when, if I could actually see myself—if I could stand inside their shoes—I might laugh too.

Recovering Pharisees need to have people around them to tell them the truth—to hold up the mirrors. This is one of the most valuable elements of the recovery-group model. By simply showing up at a meeting you are forced to encounter a different view of yourself than you have been holding most or all of your life. In a recovery group, you are putting yourself among people whom you might have formerly judged as lower than yourself. This is why showing up is the hardest part. You walk into a room full of individuals who all have a problem, and you immediately say to yourself, "I don't belong here. I'm not really this bad. These are the people who have hit bottom and have nowhere else to go. Me . . . I'm different. I'm only experimenting with this. I'm just checking it out; I won't need to be here long. After all, these are all old bald guys." Everyone starts out this way only because they have never before had a good look at that bald spot on the back of their head. Embracing this group means embracing another view of yourself.

Not just any group will do. It needs to be a group committed to telling the truth. The Pharisees traveled in a group, but it was not a group that told the truth. These kinds of groups foster a kind of collective, categorical blindness. Pharisees . . . gangs . . . Nazis . . . it's the same principle. They travel in packs with clear rules about what you talk about and what you don't. These groups replace truth with propaganda—a way of seeing the world that bolsters the false assumptions already made. You won't find any children laughing when these guys get mad. It wouldn't be tolerated.

The Pharisees always showed up together with mutual agendas, whether it was to question Jesus in order to trap him or to throw an adulterer at his feet just to see what he would do. If they were vulnerable at all to seeking the truth about Jesus, they had to go secretly, apart from the group, as Nicodemus did (John 3:1–21).

It would be wise to look at the groups we travel in and see how honest they really are. Do we have our own prejudices and secrets? Are we honest with one another, or do we protect one another's weaknesses and sins? Do our groups foster an accurate portrayal of ourselves as we really are, or do they bolster a kind of corporate lie or propaganda? Alcoholics Anonymous and "drinking buddies" are two different groups handling the same problem in entirely different ways. One group admits a problem and discloses everything in the process of rooting it out. The other group covers up the problem and similarly bolsters the cover-up by rationalizations, denials, and judgments of others as "self-righteous."

In other words, any group is a kind of mirror. The question is, is it an accurate one? We need friends who tell us the truth—other shoes in which we can stand.

There is more to this new perspective. Standing in someone else's shoes changes our view of ourselves, but it also drastically changes our view of others when we see their situation from *their* point of view. If we truly see from someone else's perspective, we might at least be able to understand why they do what they do instead of issuing a knee-jerk judgment of what we do not understand. Examples of this abound: the homosexual who was molested as a child, the abuser who was abused (almost all have been), the cruel-hearted who never knew love, the fatherless who can't father. The list goes on.

## Chapel talk

I recently spoke at a Christian college about the need for a Christian worldview, and one of the things I mentioned in passing was how listening to current popular music was a kind of "cultural listening" that was important in the process of communicating the gospel. I was at the college for three days, which included three chapel talks, and chapel attendance at this institution was required of the students. After my first talk, a student went to the chaplain and asked to be excused from my next two talks because he did not want to have to sit and listen to a speaker who would advocate listening to secular music in any form for any reason.

My first reaction was to judge him as a legalist who was not even willing to hear me out to my conclusions, but then the school chaplain informed me that he was an unusual student. He was an African-American pastor in his fifties, living in the dorms on sabbatical to earn his degree. Suddenly I began to understand. As an adult male spiritual authority figure in the African-American community, secular music to him would be the urban ghetto music of today—overt with expressions of violence, gang warfare, and the sexually explicit exploitation of women. How could anything good come of that?

Nevertheless, I would have wanted to tell the man that nothing is created out of a vacuum. This music, as painful as it is, is an indication of something the pastor/student at least must understand if he is going to seek to communicate to his culture. (He undoubtedly understood it more than I, but just didn't want to be faced with it in chapel. Chapel is where you go to get away from things like this.) Having a blanket rejection of the popular art form of his culture's youth is going to make it hard for him to have a message that relates to these kids. Kids *are* their music, and these kids are young African-American males growing up in south-central Los Angeles with most likely no father, a gang for identity, and the threat of death always nearby. What songs would I write if I were in their shoes? I don't think it would be "Love Him in the morning when you see the sun a-rising. . . ."

Had we had a chance to talk, I would have suggested that the pastor needs to listen not to be entertained, certainly, but to ask why. Why does this music exist? Why are these attitudes prevalent? What is it about life in the "hood" that fosters this anger? How can he address these problems at their root instead of simply rejecting a form of music that offends him?

There were two perspective changes necessary here. I needed to put myself in his shoes, and he needed to put himself in the shoes of these kids. I can understand why he would have a negative reaction to some white guy coming into chapel and suggesting it was a good idea to listen to secular music.

Standing in someone else's shoes would have helped us both.

## Give others the benefit of the doubt

Life can be very painful. Everyone has the same burdens, and however much you can share those burdens makes life easier for everybody. It's lonely otherwise. Every moment that you share someone else's pain, feel what they feel, makes you more human. I went through a lot of pain in my divorce. It made me feel empathy for people I don't even like, because they're going through it. I grant them all the slack I can.

This quote from a *Parade Magazine* interview with Bill Murray (February 21, 1999) is full of human insight and simple truth for recovering Pharisees. Empathy is a marvelous antidote for the tendency to judge others, and personal pain is the pathway to empathy. It's worth the pain to become more human—to identify with people—to join the human race.

Pharisees are lonely. "Perfect" people are always lonely. No one wants to be around you if you are perfect. They might fake it around you for your sake, but they will not stay long or reveal much. Other Pharisees may hang out with you, but you will still be lonely. Pharisees always protect each other from vulnerability—from being touched deeply.

Nothing touches us more deeply than pain.

A few years ago I wrote the following lyrics to a song:

*You can't bring a cup of cold water to someone*
*If you've never thirsted.*
*You can't heal a heart*
*If your heart's never been broken.*
*You can't forgive a sin that you've never done*
*Or you never thought you could do.*
*Put that bandage away—*
*It's too small to cover the wound.*
(copyright © 1999, Studio Blue Music (ASCAP), of Silent Planet)

Failure, pain, and dissatisfaction are common to us all. Pharisees pretend they do not have these things and in the process cut themselves off from the rest of the human race. Because they have attainable solutions that are currently working fine for them amid the shallow reality in which they live, they have no patience for anyone for whom these solutions are not working. They cannot empathize with anyone because they have not embraced their own shortcomings.

Bill Murray mentioned he was able to cut people some slack only because he'd faced difficult things in his own life and had an idea of what it was like. He'd come up short a few times himself and it had left him vulnerable to pain. He even said he had empathy for people he didn't like. That's a huge statement.

To empathize with someone you don't even like is a sign that you have accepted and faced your own problems and therefore can understand how other people can be trapped by their own difficulties in life, even if they are difficulties outside your experience. The woman who raced in front of me to be "next in line" at the office supply store may have had other concerns on her mind. She may have been from a large family and learned to grab for whatever she could get in order to survive. Maybe her mother had recently died and she was buying cards to notify friends and loved ones while still overcome with grief. Or maybe she was simply a very selfish person who had little or no regard for anybody around her. *Check it out, Fischer, you bastion of selflessness. Are you unable to understand that? Cut her some slack, man, even in regard to sin, if you want to be forgiven too.*

Having empathy for people you don't like is a big step for a Pharisee. If you can do it, you are on the road to recovery.

## In an A.A. meeting

Let's go back to the first time you walk into an A.A. meeting thinking that this is certainly a mistake, that this is not the right group. What happens after that?

If you stick with it, you soon find out this group is made up of people from all walks of life. There are bankers here, lawyers and doctors as well as plumbers, clerks, machinists, and the unemployed. As you listen to them talk, you begin to discover similarities in your own life—things you can't control. I am not an alcoholic but I have attended A.A. meetings and felt a strong affinity with everyone there. My particular problem may not be alcoholism, but I have something in my life that I can't control. My guess is that we all do.

As a Pharisee, there is no doubt that the need to judge other people is at the level of an addiction. It is intimately tied to our sense of identity and is the means by which we feel good about ourselves. We judge without thinking, and it's a habit we can't get along without.

Being in a room full of people like me who want to kick this habit is my best chance at changing this perspective. Suddenly I'm starting to like these people. I'm seeing myself and them in the light of the truth. I accept them. I admit my own faults they have helped me to see. There's going to come a time when I'll be willing to die for these people—the very ones I judged when I first walked into the room are now my friends.

This is the kind of thing that can happen when you start to see yourself as you really are.

*Step 1* We admit that our single most unmitigated pleasure is to judge other people.

*Step 2* Have come to believe that our means of obtaining greatness is to make everyone lower than ourselves in our own mind.

*Step 3* Realize that we detest mercy being given to those who, unlike us, haven't worked for it and don't deserve it.

*Step 4* Have decided that we don't want to get what we deserve after all, and we don't want anyone else to either.

*Step 5* Will cease all attempts to apply teaching and rebuke to anyone but ourselves.

*Step 6* Are ready to have God remove all these defects of attitude and character.

*Step 7* Embrace the belief that we are, and will always be, experts at sinning.

*Step 8* Are looking closely at the lives of famous men and women of the Bible who turned out to be ordinary sinners like us.

*Step 9* Are seeking through prayer and meditation to make a conscious effort to consider others better than ourselves.

*Step 10* Embrace the state of astonishment as a permanent and glorious reality.

*Step 11* Choose to rid ourselves of any attitude that is not bathed in gratitude.

*Step 12* Having had a spiritual awakening as the result of these steps, we will try to carry this message to others who think that Christians are better than everyone else.

STEP

# 3

*We realize that we*
*detest mercy*
*being given to those*
*who, unlike us,*
*haven't worked for it*
*and don't deserve it.*

> ( You can easily judge the character of
> others by how they treat those who can
> do nothing for them or to them.
>
> MALCOLM FORBES )

W HEN MY WIFE AND I BEGAN OUR LIFE TOGETHER IN 1975 IN
a one-bedroom cottage in the redwoods south of San
Francisco, it was with a sense of excitement on her part over
not only a new marriage but also the possibility of a unique ministry
together with me. As a flight attendant and a new Christian, she had
risen rapidly to a position of leadership as founder and director of a Los
Angeles-based organization for Christian flight attendants, pilots,
mechanics, ticket agents, and management. This was during the
influence of the Jesus movement, and the same kind of spiritual hunger
that brought young people flocking to church also was at work in the
airline industry. Our meeting and courtship was not only a time of
falling in love but also of mutual respect for what God was doing in
each other's lives. We were two spiritual leaders coming together in
partnership—at least that was the way Marti saw it. Thus it was with a
great deal of surprise and disappointment that she quickly discovered
her vision of our ministry together was not exactly shared by her
husband.

Though Marti had been schooled in Hal Lindsey's Jesus Christ
Light and Power House training center in Westwood, California, I had
been an intern in the teaching and discipling program of Peninsula Bible
Church in Palo Alto under the direction of Ray Stedman and other

pastors. We were convinced our program was the only one in the nation like it, and the fact that pastors from all over the country were coming to learn from our model was evidence of that fact. In many ways we were the "Willow Creek" of the '70s. It was the feeling of my pastors and me at the time that even though God had obviously used Marti in a significant way in her first four years as a Christian, it was now time to put her ministry "on the shelf" for a season and do some serious study to promote her own spiritual growth.

Though I failed to see this as a pharisaical act at the time, I now view it as fraught with spiritual pride and envy. I needed to ensure I was spiritually superior to my wife. *Wasn't that the biblical way?* I needed to make certain my ministry was more visible than hers. So the woman who organized evangelistic events, taught Bible studies, and appeared in pulpits and on radio and television across the country was now going to settle down to being a good little Christian "wifey."

It was inconceivable to me that the spiritual training I had worked so hard for could be so easily gifted to someone else, and someone from a pagan background, no less. Well, perhaps it had been a gift for a specific time and purpose, but now that we had the rest of our lives ahead of us, it was time for her to put ministry on hold and do the necessary work to catch up with me. Maybe she eventually could work up to a small discipleship group of women.

I have come to regret this action and the subsequent ministry together that I forfeited because of it. For if there was supposed to be a time when this "training" period was completed, it never came. I continued in my own directions and Marti eventually took off on hers, demonstrating through her gifts of leadership and encouragement a ministry written on her heart and displayed through her life to people who, as she would put it, "have yet to accept the Lord."

Working for something and deserving it are near and dear to a Pharisee's heart. Earning and deserving, punishments and rewards, are the matters that make up a pharisaical life. Unfortunately these are the very things that hinder the enjoyment and appreciation of God and his gifts. Pharisees actually do get what they deserve, which may seem like a lot, but in reality it never amounts to much in this lifetime and tragically ends with nothing that will survive the fires of judgment in the next. It's a very costly error.

In the parable of the workers in the vineyard (Matthew 20:1–16), a landowner went out in the morning and hired some men to work in his vineyard for an agreed-upon sum of money. As the day wore on the landowner needed more workers, so he went out and hired additional men at various times of the day right up until the eleventh hour. When evening came, he instructed his foreman to pay the workers their wages "beginning with the last ones hired and going on to the first."

Fair enough. Fine so far. But when the ones who were hired first stood around and watched what others were getting paid, they found out everybody was getting the same amount—the amount they had agreed upon at the start of the day.

Now, just a minute here! "These men who were hired last worked only one hour," they said to the foreman, "and you have made them equal to us who have borne the burden of the work and the heat of the day."

On the surface, it is a totally understandable gripe; it does seem unfair that workers with unequal time were paid the same. But their gripe would never fly with the Better Business Bureau, because the employer fulfilled his contract. They got the amount for which they consented to work. What the other laborers received was the prerogative of the landowner.

"Friend, I am not being unfair to you," the landowner told one of the first workers, who was grumbling against him. "Didn't you agree to work for a denarius? Take your pay and go. I want to give the man who was hired last the same as I gave you. Don't I have the right to do what I want with my own money? Or are you envious because I am generous?"

Like many of the parables of Jesus, this one was told primarily for the benefit of the Pharisees. They would have recognized themselves right off as the first workers in this story because they had been working their whole lives to earn their reward, and they prided themselves in their heritage going back to Moses, the law, and the prophets. They were the ones in charge of the holy things—doling them out to those who were deserving and holding them back from those who, in their opinion, were not. The later workers were the poor and the lame and the blind and the leprous and the publicans and the sinners—the last on the scene—in short, the riffraff that seemed to gather around Jesus wherever he went like the cloud of dirt around Charles Schulz's Pig Pen (of "Peanuts" cartoon fame). The Pharisees could never accept that what they had worked so hard for, someone else could get for almost nothing, especially someone outside the boundaries of their cherished traditions.

They also were obvious purveyors of Step 2, priding themselves in being better than those without the law and traditions. Jesus knew their hearts and voiced their attitude through the mouths of the first workers in his parable: "You have made them equal to us." It was not only equal pay they were bothered about; it was equal worth and personhood. The Pharisees could not stand being put on the same level as everyone else. It was unthinkable.

The last point Jesus makes in the parable is perhaps the most difficult of all for Pharisees to understand. He refers to the vast, glorious, and sometimes reckless generosity of God. If they could have only comprehended this generosity and accepted God as he is, they could have received him for themselves. It was their pride that kept them from seeing.

God's grace makes level ground. Sin evens the playing field so grace can abound to all. The generosity of God knows no bounds and is no respecter of persons. If your whole system is built on respecting some people over others, then the grace of God will not be a welcome thing to you because it flows unequivocally to everybody. Imagine hearing that *all* people who repent of their sin and turn to Christ can have every spiritual thing you have been working for so diligently, and that they can have it immediately by faith. It hardly seems fair. It would be difficult to handle. To some of us it is.

Jesus was announcing that the kingdom of God had come, and it had come to a small band of fishermen and common people. It was being heartily received by the poor and the blind, the publicans and the sinners, seemingly anyone fool enough to believe it—all of them completely uninitiated in the necessary traditions and religious practices the Pharisees spent all their efforts guarding. No wonder this was not good news to them. Suddenly everybody's getting paid the same thing. Scoundrels are getting ushered into the kingdom of God.

The first workers had no gripe about their own pay; it was the other guy's pay that bothered them. So it will always be with Pharisees.

## "She works hard for the money. . . ."

I can also imagine some of those workers who got paid a full day's wage for one hour of work walking away saying, "Do you think that foreman made a mistake?" And the natural human response would be, "I don't want to know."

The point isn't dishonesty; we're not speaking of something wrongly taken but rather grace freely offered. When you've gotten more than you deserve, you don't want to talk about what you deserve anymore. You know if you got what you deserved it would be less than this.

It is this way with God's grace. People who have received it don't care anymore about measurements; they know how it would turn out if they started counting. They obviously have received more than they deserve. They're just happy to take it, and they don't really care what amount anybody else gets either. "Take your pay and go," Jesus said to the Pharisees, which was exactly what the other workers did—they pocketed the money and kept their mouths shut about measurements and scales and rules and standards. They knew that if things were truly counted out, they would have to give back most of what they had received.

This is the same thing Jesus is talking about when, in the Gospels of Mark, Luke, and twice in Matthew, he says, "Whoever has will be given more; whoever does not have, even what he thinks he has will be taken from him" (Luke 8:18).

The person who "has" is the person who has received freely from God. The person who "thinks he has" is the person who has worked hard for his spiritual status. He has gotten what is rightfully his and thinks he deserves it. This is what so deeply irked the Pharisees about Jesus and why they could never believe in him. To believe in Jesus, they would have to have given up their connection between work and pay. They would have to have lost the whole system by which they had established their identity, their sense of worth, and their standing among men that they thought separated themselves from the scum of the earth.

Jesus was always telling the Pharisees they had their reward already, and that was actually the way they wanted it. In contrast, he always told believers that they would have in abundance, and after that, more was on the way. We have a generous God; unfortunately Pharisees don't know that and don't want to know.

Pharisees always get what they bargain for; recovering Pharisees get more. Pharisees make it their business to measure themselves and everybody around them; recovering Pharisees have learned to avoid that subject entirely and simply receive with a thankful heart what God gives them.

## The "law" of the Pharisees

Once again this brings up the issue of control. Pharisees want control of the rules of the game so they can ensure their place in it. If they control the rules, they can make sure they are "in" while undesirables stay "out." God's mercy, given freely to those who haven't worked for it and don't deserve it, is a threat to that control. It undermines everything.

These rules, of course, are not the actual laws of God; they are interpretations of the law. For instance, the Pharisees in Jesus' time had a long list of things they could and could not do on the Sabbath. Many of these things were not in the law of Moses. They were a sort of unofficial "law" of the Pharisees.

As previously mentioned, Christians today have similar lists built more on tradition than on the intent of the law. Many Christians believe they are Christians by doing and/or not doing certain things. These things usually deal with cultural issues that are not even mentioned in the Bible, and Christians spend a good deal of time absorbed in "defining" these things and then priding themselves for obeying them and condemning those who don't. This reinterpretation of the law is a pharisaical necessity because, properly interpreted, as was done by Jesus, the law would convict *everyone*, including Pharisees. But if the law can be reduced to cultural or sabbatical practices, which some engage in and some do not, then we once again can be "in control" of spirituality.

## Impossible for most but possible for some

This brings up another means by which Pharisees maintain control over spirituality: slightly altering the definition of sin. It requires some delicate maneuvering. The important thing is to make sin something that can't be avoided except by a careful exertion of human effort. The line needs to be drawn in a critical place, far enough out to implicate most people while not too far for Pharisees themselves to reach. "Impossible for most, but possible for some"—that could be the motto of pharisaical spirituality.

The Pharisees of Jesus' day accomplished this neat trick primarily by focusing on certain "big" and "little" sins, the avoidance of which separated them from the rest of humanity and gave them what they thought was a superior position. I will call these *macro* and *micro* sins. In foiling both of these, Jesus revealed the Pharisees' deception and unmasked their power.

*Macro sins.* These are sins that generally can be avoided most of the time by most of us without too much effort. They are pretty much laid out in the Ten Commandments, handed down through Moses on tablets of stone. Things like adultery, murder, stealing, and coveting your neighbor's possessions are things that can be avoided at least outwardly with a reasonable amount of effort (and probably a dash of hypocrisy). The Pharisees could avoid adultery, not murder anyone, fudge on divorce because Moses allowed it (Matthew 19), and even love their neighbor by hating their enemies and justifying it through non-didactic Scriptures like Psalm 139:21–22: "Do I not hate those who hate you, O Lord, and abhor those who rise up against you? I have nothing but hatred for them; I count them my enemies."

In like manner, many pharisaical Christians can steer clear of "big" sins without too much sacrifice. This is the first level of elimination that separates Christians from a fairly large segment of the population.

*Micro sins.* At the same time Pharisees draw other sins out to the nth degree. Many of these are not even announced to everyone. They are special sins that Pharisees construct—practices that non-Pharisees are violating without knowing it because they never heard of the rule (or more likely they don't care).

Here's an example. "The Pharisees and all the Jews do not eat unless they give their hands a ceremonial washing, holding to the traditions of the elders. When they come from the marketplace they do not eat unless they wash. And they observe many other traditions, such as the washing of cups, pitchers and kettles" (Mark 7:3–4). These are micro sins to which Jesus replied, "You have a fine way of setting aside the commands of God in order to observe your own traditions!" (Mark 7:9).

Washing cups, pitchers, and kettles? Who cares? Only the Pharisees. Which is exactly why this little trick works so well. Not only do these traditions separate the Pharisee from the rest of humanity, they allow the Pharisee to deflect the larger issues of love, mercy, and justice by being consumed with irrelevant minutiae.

To both of these definitions Jesus delivered crushing blows. For the macro sins he reinterpreted them through the eyes of the heart. He showed the Pharisees that while they prided themselves over publicly abstaining from adultery and murder, in their hearts they were violating the real intent of the law through lust and hatred.

And then he showed that in their attention to micro sins they were again missing the bigger point. Pharisees are the religious leaders who would make allowances to rescue sheep that might fall into a pit on the Sabbath in order to protect their personal property, but would call sinful the healing of a human being on the same day (Matthew 12:9–12). Jesus called this "straining at gnats" while "swallowing camels." This is the practice of engineering sins to a size one can control while missing all the huge implications of the deeds, thoughts, and intents of the heart.

But Pharisees want more than control over the definition of sin. They want control of the holy things themselves. They set themselves up as the holy ones who have the inside track on God. They want people to come to them to get to God. *This has always been the great temptation of spiritual position outside of the grace of God.* What could be more tantalizing than having a God whose position you can assume and whose power you can manipulate? Like the Wizard of Oz, Pharisees erect a god ominous and powerful and bigger than everybody and then go behind the facade and control it from the inside so as to make themselves its high and lofty representatives and the people their spiritual subjects. This is the heart of the system of religion Jesus detests and will ultimately destroy.

## Mercy is out of control

No wonder the Pharisees wanted to kill Jesus. They had their tentacles around so many people and they had control of the holy things and the holy places. Jesus came along and threatened it all. He brought the kingdom of God directly to the commoners and made God's power available to everyone through faith.

He made heroes out of ordinary people and conspicuously left out the Pharisees. Fishermen, tax collectors, prostitutes, Roman soldiers, housewives, children, the blind, the lame, and the deranged were the people Jesus honored. Generally they were an undeserving lot who had earned no spiritual status, and yet they were the entourage of the Son of God. To all of them, Jesus had the audacity to say, "The kingdom of God is within you" (Luke 17:21).

The Pharisees never got over this. These people were lowlifes to them—the dregs of humanity. They wouldn't even want a place in heaven if it were to include these folks.

The biggest blow to all of this nonsense came when God moved to forgive everybody and put salvation on the basis of faith alone. God's mercy pulls the rug out from under everything a Pharisee has worked for and prided himself in. If Jesus was right, there was no need for a Pharisee. Nothing for a Pharisee to do. Enter the wild and wacky and unpredictable—even unfair—mercy of God. A mercy that puts everyone on the same level. There are no spiritual stages in mercy. There are no mediators. There are no big sins and little sins. The mercy of God is God's business, and I have nothing to say about who gets it and who doesn't except to be overjoyed that I, for reasons unknown to me, am one who does.

## Giving up control

Just as control is so important to the Pharisee, it must be completely and utterly relinquished in order to recover what God intended for us. Control very well could be the Pharisee's main addiction. Control means I get to work for and deserve what I get from God for the very reason that I am controlling it.

There is really only one cure to this addiction: (1) to realize who God is and how beyond our control are his ways, (2) to see that the end of what we work for apart from him is all without worth, and (3) to accept that there is nothing for us to measure except the immeasurable grace of God—no one to compare ourselves to but Christ.

The first is what leads us to worship, the second is what leads us to depend on him for everything, and the third is what unites us with everyone else.

Worship is a relinquishing of control. The essence of worship is to admit that we are not God and never really wanted to be in the first place, though we may have acted like it for a while. We are happy to find our place as his subjects, and we bow down and worship him in the beauty of his holiness. In this place we forget all about ourselves. We are swallowed up in his greatness. John the Baptist explained that his joy was made complete in becoming smaller while Christ was continually enlarged in his vision (John 3:30).

This is when we are happiest, when *God* receives praise, not us. What we were made to do, in the words of the Westminster Catechism of the Presbyterian Church, is "to glorify God and enjoy Him forever." That enjoyment comes in finding our rightful place by putting God in his. Of course we do not "put" God anywhere—he is already there—

but in worshiping him, we are acknowledging where he belongs, and where we belong in relationship to him.

In this place of worship we sense that we do not deserve to be here. We haven't worked for this and we have not earned any right to stand before a holy God. In fact, we are acutely and painfully aware, in his presence, of our unholiness. The closer we get to God, the more unworthy we feel and the more amazed we are that he accepts us and receives our praise and would actually want to use us to help achieve his purposes in the world. All of this happens when we truly worship the only living God.

But good works are also a relinquishing of control. To accomplish anything worthy of the kingdom of God, we must give up our need to control the spiritual aspects of our lives. We lay down, as it were, our pharisaical robes and realize that we cannot do anything for God unless he is working in and through us. We accomplish nothing in our own strength; we only mess things up as the Pharisees did.

Paul said, "If any man builds on this foundation using gold, silver, costly stones, wood, hay or straw, his work will be shown for what it is, because the Day will bring it to light. It will be revealed with fire, and the fire will test the quality of each man's work" (1 Corinthians 3:12–13). There is therefore a quality of work at issue here—work that will burn up and work that will survive the test. The key to what survives is the foundation on which the works are built: "For no one can lay any foundation other than the one already laid, which is Jesus Christ" (v. 11).

The Pharisees were known for their "works." They were constantly maintaining their spiritual status, working their way to an impressive place before God and the people. But according to Paul, their work will burn up in the fire of the final judgment because it was not work built on the foundation of Jesus Christ. If they'd built on a foundation of faith, which, by the way, Paul would say was available to them as it was to their father, Abraham (see Romans 5), they would have recognized Jesus as the Son of God—the Word on whom they had been depending all along. Instead of recognizing him, they killed him for the very reason that he was a threat to their system of works apart from him.

In the same way, we can be religious and do all sorts of things for God, but if these are not done in humble dependence on Christ, they will amount to nothing. We need to relinquish our control over "what we do for God," and trust wholly in what God does in and through us as we live and walk by faith.

Finally, our worth is also found in relinquishing control of our spiritual image or reputation. Our worth comes in joining the rest of the human race—in coming down off our spiritual pedestals and giving up the constant attempt to establish our value in comparison to other people.

Our value comes in being made in the image of God, in being the recipient of the love of the God who went to the cross for us. These things are true for everyone, not just Christians. We are special, but not more special than any other human being in God's eyes. Again, we accept that there is nothing for us to measure except for the immeasurable grace of God. No one to compare ourselves to but Christ.

And now for one final look at those guys walking away with a full day's pay for one hour of work: Do they care what other people got? Are they snooping around other people's paychecks to make sure everything's equitable and fair? I doubt it. If you've been given mercy, you don't care who else gets it. Give it to the whole world for all you care, you are so thankful that *you* got it.

But if you earned it, the opposite is true. If you earned it, you care. You care a lot. You care because you don't want anybody getting paid who hasn't worked as hard as you. You don't want anybody getting off easy. And if it bothers you that someone does, then chances are you're counting on something other than mercy to make you acceptable to God.

*Step 1* We admit that our single most unmitigated pleasure is to judge other people.

*Step 2* Have come to believe that our means of obtaining greatness is to make everyone lower than ourselves in our own mind.

*Step 3* Realize that we detest mercy being given to those who, unlike us, haven't worked for it and don't deserve it.

*Step 4* Have decided that we don't want to get what we deserve after all, and we don't want anyone else to either.

*Step 5* Will cease all attempts to apply teaching and rebuke to anyone but ourselves.

*Step 6* Are ready to have God remove all these defects of attitude and character.

*Step 7* Embrace the belief that we are, and will always be, experts at sinning.

*Step 8* Are looking closely at the lives of famous men and women of the Bible who turned out to be ordinary sinners like us.

*Step 9* Are seeking through prayer and meditation to make a conscious effort to consider others better than ourselves.

*Step 10* Embrace the state of astonishment as a permanent and glorious reality.

*Step 11* Choose to rid ourselves of any attitude that is not bathed in gratitude.

*Step 12* Having had a spiritual awakening as the result of these steps, we will try to carry this message to others who think that Christians are better than everyone else.

STEP

*We have decided that
we don't want to get
what we deserve
after all, and
we don't want
anyone else to either.*

> ( When you stand at the Pearly Gates,
> would you rather be told that you were
> too forgiving or you were too judgmental? )
>
> L E O N A R D   S W E E T

---

I CAME HOME FROM THE SECOND GRADE ONE DAY DISTRAUGHT OVER a check on my report card for talking in class. Now, that doesn't seem like an impeachable offense, except that it was not the first time I had earned an unsatisfactory citizenship grade. I had, in fact, received two or three of these on consecutive report cards, and my parents had threatened me with the switch if I brought home one more bad mark.

The switch wouldn't have been half as bad if I had ever received it, but up until then it had only been threatened as a last resort, and so far, the mere mention of it was enough to make me straighten up. With each successive threat, its portent had grown significantly more ominous in my mind. Now there was no avoiding it. It was done. The check was on the card. In ink. There was nothing I could do about it. I bore in my hands the sealing of my fate.

By the time I completed my walk home from school I was an emotional wreck. I delayed as long as I could so that when I came through the door I was hyperventilating from crying so much. My parents rushed to me when they heard me come in and wanted to know what on earth had happened. They thought I had gotten into a fight or an accident. I handed them my report card and waited for doomsday. I remember my mother eyeing my father with slight amusement and a this-was-your-idea-you-deal-with-it sort of look. They went to another room to discuss my sentence and I heard my mother saying, "Hasn't he suffered enough already?" and my dad saying something like, "We have to follow through on this or else our word means nothing."

So I got the switch, and it wasn't quite as bad as I had made it out to be in my mind, but it was bad enough.

My father felt in this case that it was necessary to uphold his word and carry out the judgment so as not to take the edge off of future threats. If he let me get away with this, what would I be into next? But I think now, being on the other end of parenting, that he had other options that perhaps he didn't see.

Another possibility would have been to say, "Son, you deserve the switch, but I'm not going to go through with it this time. Instead, I am going to extend something to you that is called *mercy*. It's what God gives us many times instead of punishing us. You deserve the switch because I told you this was the standard if you brought home a bad report, but I'm going to give you mercy instead because my love for you is bigger than the standard."

"Mercy" as it is translated in the Old Testament refers to God's faithfulness to a graciously established relationship with Israel despite human unworthiness and defection. It is a steady, persistent refusal of God to wash his hands of a wayward people. Time and time again we see God reneging on his vow to rid the earth of these disobedient, murmuring, ungrateful children, even though he would have been justified in doing so. If God's justice had not been tempered with his mercy, the children of Israel would never have made it any farther than the other side of the Red Sea.

But God is a merciful God. Even in the midst of his consummate rendering of the law in the Ten Commandments we find a statement of his kindness: "I, the Lord your God, am a jealous God, punishing the children for the sin of the fathers to the third and fourth generation of those who hate me, but showing love to a thousand generations of those who love me and keep my commandments" (Exodus 20:5-6).

God is both just and merciful, and there should be no doubt here which one of those qualities he favors. He leans toward kindness a thousand to four. Those are pretty good odds and every bit necessary when you consider how stubborn and disobedient we are.

" 'The Lord is slow to anger, abounding in love and forgiving sin and rebellion. . . . ' In accordance with your great love, forgive the sin of these people, just as you have pardoned them from the time they left Egypt until now" (Numbers 14:18–19).

This was one of Moses' many prayers to God on behalf of an unfaithful nation, and a prayer where he appeals to God's generous love in spite of their sin and rebellion. Eight other times in the Old Testament the phrase "slow to anger" is applied to God, and each of these references is accompanied by qualities such as abundant love, faithfulness, and compassion.

What's more, this is the Old Testament, with an Old Testament God known for his wrath and vindication. Christ hasn't come yet; the final sacrifice has not been paid, and yet we still see his love and patience dominating.

"He does not treat us as our sins deserve or repay us according to our iniquities" (Psalm 103:10). "The Lord is good to all; he has compassion on all he has made" (Psalm 145:9). That last verse indicates there is a compassion God bestows on *all* his creation. He is not merely compassionate to those who believe in him and belong to him. He has compassion on all. This is what is generally called "common grace," and all creation shares in it. This is what allows people to experience a level of joy and goodness in their lives regardless of their faith in God. This goodness is sometimes a threat to pharisaical Christians, who often try to discredit it as a challenge to their own goodness (which must remain superior).

## The day of salvation

If God's Old Testament mercy is surprising, then his New Testament mercy is overwhelmingly stunning.

We live in a mixed-up age, where righteousness and evil, wheat and tares grow up together. Our response to this disoriented world is one of the biggest challenges we face as Christians. There are many Christian Pharisees who want to bring judgment upon this world right now. They want to see justice done. They want to see God get even. Like Jonah, they want the fire to come down and consume Nineveh, or at least San Francisco. They want people to get what they deserve. But it's not going to happen.

It's not going to happen because Jesus and Peter and Paul already told us it's not going to happen. All three of them told us this is not the day of judgment; it is the day of salvation.

When Jesus read in the temple from the prophecy of Isaiah about being anointed to preach good news to the poor and offer freedom to the captives and give sight to the blind and release the oppressed and then proclaimed those dramatic words: "Today this scripture is fulfilled in your hearing," he actually stopped in the middle of Isaiah's sentence. He closed the scroll right after he read, "to proclaim the year of the Lord's favor." The experts in Old Testament prophecy would have recognized that it was a purposeful exclusion—a conspicuous omission. The Isaiahic passage goes on to mention ". . . and the day of vengeance of our God." But Jesus did not read that part. He stopped before he read about God getting even. Again, that is because this is not the age in which people get what they deserve. It is the age of salvation.

Listen to this: It better not be the day of judgment, because if it were, you wouldn't be reading this book and I wouldn't be writing it. Here's why:

> You, therefore, have no excuse, you who pass judgment on someone else, for at whatever point you judge the other, you are condemning yourself, because you who pass judgment do the same things. Now we know that God's judgment against those who do such things is based on truth. So when you, a mere man, pass judgment on them and yet do the same things, do you think you will escape God's judgment? Or do you show contempt for the riches of his kindness, tolerance and patience, not realizing that God's kindness leads you toward repentance?
>
> But because of your stubbornness and your unrepentant heart, you are storing up wrath against yourself for the day of

God's wrath, when his righteous judgment will be revealed. (Romans 2:1–5)

We are "storing up wrath" when we condemn others, because this is a time in history when God is overlooking these things so he can attend to the salvation of as many as possible. Yes, this means you can get away with sin now, and you can also get away with judging, too, but only for a while. It mounts up. It goes somewhere, and it will all come back.

"Bear in mind," wrote Peter, "that our Lord's patience means salvation" (2 Peter 3:15). The longer he waits, the more who can be saved. That means every day we continue to live with lies, disobedience, and evil seemingly unchecked is also a day for someone to be saved. Instead of lamenting how horrible the world is getting, Christians should be marveling at the mercy of God that lets it go on. There is a reason for his restraint. This is the day of salvation.

And this is exactly what is supposed to be happening. Righteousness and evil growing up next to each other. Unthinkable sins going unpunished. People getting away with murder. Yet people getting saved as well. That is what this age is all about.

And yet we go around condemning sinners and trying to fix the world. Listen: The world isn't supposed to get fixed; people are supposed to get saved! "Now is the time of God's favor," Paul picked up the theme as well, "now is the day of salvation" (2 Corinthians 6:2).

"The Lord is not slow in keeping his promise, as some understand slowness. He is patient with you, not wanting anyone to perish, but everyone to come to repentance" (2 Peter 3:9). This is the heart of God. He doesn't want anyone to perish. Though it is what every one of us deserves, he does not want to have to carry it out. He therefore has punished his Son in our place so he doesn't have to carry out our punishment.

Yet not everyone comprehends it. Not everyone has heard, and even some of those who have heard still don't get it because they heard it wrong or we told them wrong. That's what this age is for: to get the news out and get it right.

## You deserve a break today

Judgment is not going to happen now, and as much as you or I might wish for it on others, I don't think we really want it to happen now. If other people got what they deserved, then we would have to get it too, and unless you particularly like the thought of burning with a heat that will boil your skin and leave you light-years away from love and truth and light, forever shrieking out into the darkness of nothing, I suggest not bringing it up.

James wrote, "Speak and act as those who are going to be judged by the law that gives freedom, because judgment without mercy will be shown to anyone who has not been merciful. Mercy triumphs over judgment!" (James 2:12–13).

There is a law that brings freedom, and that is the law of mercy that triumphs over judgment. This is not a "cheap grace," mind you; it was bought at the price of God's Son on a cross. But if you have received it, you will want to be giving it out as well. *Receiving mercy yourself and being merciful to others always go hand in hand. You cannot have one without the other.*

Now is the time to focus in on the riches of God's kindness, tolerance, and patience and leave the judgment to another day and another Judge.

## Getting even

The prophet Jonah wanted the people of Nineveh to get what they deserved. He wanted it so badly that he refused to go to warn them of God's coming judgment, because he had a hunch they might actually heed his warning and repent and God would be merciful instead. He knew God that well.

"That is why I was so quick to flee to Tarshish," he said, after God turned him around and sent him to Nineveh anyway. "I knew that you are a gracious and compassionate God, slow to anger and abounding in love, a God who relents from sending calamity" (Jonah 4:2).

Jonah still felt this way after what he dreaded came true and the people repented and God had mercy on them. Like a prophet of doom without a job description, he went off and sulked about it for days. Jonah must have had some bitter enemies in Nineveh to have felt this strongly about their judgment.

Sometimes I wonder if as Christians we can fall into similar attitudes, preferring the destruction of our enemies over their salvation. I wonder what would happen if for some mysterious reason all the perceived enemies of Christians in America right now—the pro-choice supporters, gay rights activists, militant feminists, and secular humanists, to name a few—suddenly ended up in church. What if God decided to give them all a soft heart toward him? What would we do? How would we react? Would this be cause for great rejoicing, or would we go off and sulk somewhere like Jonah?

Even more, would we be out of a job? Have we as Christians so identified ourselves with moral indignation and the antagonistic side of a right-and-wrong battle that we have no place in our hearts for God's mercy and compassion? What would we do if there was no one to be mad at anymore? Are we so invested in being antagonistic toward elements of society that appall us that we have forsaken our calling as ambassadors of reconciliation to a lost world? (See 2 Corinthians 5:17–20.)

Those who have been saved by the cross of Christ have no other business with the world than to carry the blessed news of their salvation to other offenders, regardless of the offense. Any other attitude simply does not belong among the redeemed.

If we are uncomfortable associating with sinners, then we might want to think twice about spending eternity in heaven. Heaven is for sinners who face their sin; hell is for those who refuse to see. One of the ironic similarities between heaven and hell is that no one in either place thinks they got what they deserve.

We need to relinquish any thoughts of getting even with our enemies. Jesus called us to a higher road—to love our enemies—to warn them about the coming judgment, not to see them judged.

Jonah sat down and sulked over the repentance of Nineveh. He sulked over a merciful, compassionate God who decided not to give wicked people their due. One measly little step toward him and he stayed his vengeful hand. Well, Jonah certainly wasn't going to stick around for this miserably happy moment in the history of the wicked city of Nineveh, especially after God made him out to be a liar. So Jonah made himself a little place to sit on a hillside overlooking the city and waited to see what would happen, though he was afraid it would be nothing. While he sat there brooding in the hot sun, God caused a vine to grow up over him and give him shade. And Jonah was happy about the vine. The next day God withered the vine, and in the hot sun with no relief, Jonah decided he wanted to die.

"Do you have a right to be angry about the vine?" God asked.

"I do," answered Jonah. Jonah felt he had good reason to be angry about lots of things right then.

But the Lord said, "You have been concerned about this vine, though you did not tend it or make it grow. It sprang up overnight and died overnight. But Nineveh has more than a hundred and twenty thousand people who cannot tell their right hand from their left, and many cattle as well. Should I not be concerned about that great city?" (Jonah 4:9–11).

If God was concerned about 120,000 ignorant people and a bunch of cattle, we can assume he is equally concerned about our wicked and troubled generation as well as our ailing planet and its endangered species. Instead of being known by that same world as vengeful moralists ready to pounce on the nearest enemy of our religious rights, wouldn't it go well with our position as representatives of our Savior to be known instead as those who, like our God, are "gracious and compassionate, slow to anger and abounding in love"? Our first thought should be that our enemies might repent and receive the same mercy that God has shown us.

## Rescue the perishing

Shortly after the turn of the twentieth century Fanny Crosby wrote a hymn reflecting an attitude that has all but disappeared in the church. In this hymn we glimpse the sinner as victim, trapped in the grip of the tempter, sinning and insulting a God who nonetheless remains patient and kind, ready to administer forgiveness and mercy at the slightest indication of a repentant heart. The attitude such a picture fosters in the believer is not one of judgment, but of pity. It's an attitude that calls for kindness, compassion, patience, and gentleness toward those who do not believe. There is no talk of judgment, no mood of condemnation, other than the implied judgment of God that compels the Christian toward the unsaved. They are perishing and *will* perish in their sins but for the grace of God that can awaken, restore, and lift up.

Thus the writer and, consequently, singer of this hymn is not far from danger herself. When she bids us snatch the sinner from sin and the grave, it is because she herself has been duly snatched from her own fatal predicament. She has received mercy at the hands of a merciful God. She is therefore ready and eager to extend that mercy even to the most rebellious of sinners. She knows that there is no one beyond the reach of his grace, no one outside the realm of his mercy. Believe me, we don't want what we deserve. We want what God gives to all undeserving sinners who turn to him to be saved.

> *Rescue the perishing, care for the dying,*
> *Snatch them in pity from sin and the grave;*
> *Weep o'er the erring one, lift up the fallen.*
> *Tell them of Jesus the mighty to save.*
> *Rescue the perishing, care for the dying;*
> *Jesus is merciful, Jesus will save.*
>
> *Though they are slighting Him, still He is waiting,*
> *Waiting the penitent child to receive;*
> *Plead with them earnestly, plead with them gently,*
> *He will forgive if they only believe.*
>
> *Down in the human heart, crushed by the tempter,*
> *Feelings lie buried that grace can restore;*
> *Touched by a loving heart, wakened by kindness,*
> *Chords that were broken will vibrate once more.*
>
> *Rescue the perishing, duty demands it;*
> *Strength for thy labor the Lord will provide.*

*Back to the narrow way patiently win them;*
*Tell the poor wanderer a Savior has died.*

I'm sure that when I get to heaven, I will run into people I never expected to see there. I'll bet it will be the same for you. It will be, I think, like the big party the king threw at his palace that received a poor reception among all the bigwigs and VIPs who got invitations but didn't even bother to show up or RSVP. It will be like the parable Jesus told that had the king sending out his servants at the last minute to round up whomever they could drum up from the streets and surrounding neighborhoods to take the places of all those Pharisees who had better things to do.

**Step 1** We admit that our single most unmitigated pleasure is to judge other people.

**Step 2** Have come to believe that our means of obtaining greatness is to make everyone lower than ourselves in our own mind.

**Step 3** Realize that we detest mercy being given to those who, unlike us, haven't worked for it and don't deserve it.

**Step 4** Have decided that we don't want to get what we deserve after all, and we don't want anyone else to either.

**Step 5** Will cease all attempts to apply teaching and rebuke to anyone but ourselves.

**Step 6** Are ready to have God remove all these defects of attitude and character.

**Step 7** Embrace the belief that we are, and will always be, experts at sinning.

**Step 8** Are looking closely at the lives of famous men and women of the Bible who turned out to be ordinary sinners like us.

**Step 9** Are seeking through prayer and meditation to make a conscious effort to consider others better than ourselves.

**Step 10** Embrace the state of astonishment as a permanent and glorious reality.

**Step 11** Choose to rid ourselves of any attitude that is not bathed in gratitude.

**Step 12** Having had a spiritual awakening as the result of these steps, we will try to carry this message to others who think that Christians are better than everyone else.

S T E P

We will cease all
attempts to apply
teaching and rebuke
to anyone but
ourselves.

> Not my brother, not my sister,
> but it's me, O Lord,
> Standin' in the need of prayer.
>
> TRADITIONAL SPIRITUAL

PHARISEES HAVE A HABIT OF APPLYING TRUTH TO EVERYONE BUT themselves. Someone is undoubtedly reading this book with someone else in mind. We all have ways of avoiding scrutiny when the truth comes our way. We are masters of deflection.

"That was a great message for my son, do you have it on tape?"

"My daughter needs to hear this."

"This would be a wonderful book for my husband."

"What would JoAnne think of this, I wonder?"

I can't tell you how many times in my career in contemporary Christian music parents have come up to me after I finished pouring out my heart and soul trying to reach them, and said, "I'm so glad you're doing this music for the kids."

We see clearly what others need while huge blind spots prevent us from seeing our own vulnerability. Like the weak-willed in faith that Paul warned Timothy about who were "always learning but never able to acknowledge the truth" (2 Timothy 3:7), we hear it but never take it in and apply it to our lives. Yet we seem to have no problem hearing it for everyone else.

## Judging those who judge

One of the clearest examples of this has become apparent to me in the writing of this book. I have found that in seeking to identify pharisaical attitudes, I have found them in others more easily than in myself.

For instance, in the last few years I have become increasingly critical of what I see as a prevailing attitude among Christians toward the world. I have been concerned that in choosing a moral/political banner to wave, the church has alienated the unsaved from the very message that will save them. I have also noticed that whenever I write about this or talk about it, I get angry. My writing, for instance, has to go through a number of revisions before I have calmed it down to where it might help someone think instead of merely react defensively to me. It takes a day or two for the smoke to clear. My own best critic, my wife, has caught me on my high horse too many times to mention.

So here I am getting angry at Christians for getting angry at the world. Slowly and painfully I realize that I, the one who is on a crusade to stop Christians from condemning the world, am doing the same thing by condemning judgmental Christians. What's the difference? I am judging the "judgers," and which is worse? The one that I can do something about: myself.

It's so subtle the way this hypocrisy creeps in. It starts by thinking you are an expert on something—that you know more than others, at least about certain things. In this case, the thing I imagine I know more about is everyone's judgmental attitude. Think of the irony in that. How far does this go? I wonder if you are now judging me for judging Christians for judging. If you are, you can be sure that if I hear of it, I will judge you for judging me for judging Christians for judging.

## The buck stops here

How does one stop this merry-go-round of condemnation? The only way to stop it is to apply the truth to ourselves. Realize that whatever we are angry about in someone else is most likely something we need to deal with in our own lives. That is one of the primary reasons we see the problem in the first place, because it is, first, our problem. It's just that it is easier to recognize in someone else. Easier to point the finger than to face the truth. Easier to see out than to see in.

I could not write this book if I were not an expert on being a

Pharisee. I could not speak about judging if I did not have a problem with it. And when I do speak, I can sense my voice mounting as I go.

It's been said that when the preacher shouts, it's because of a personal struggle with the issue at hand. You get worked up over what you are battling in your own life. I have found this to be painfully true. I have sat down from speaking with my voice still ringing in my ears and felt the stinging truth inside. *It's me I'm going after so ruthlessly. It's my confusion I'm trying to unravel. It's my fear I'm trying to assuage. It's my judging I'm trying to stop. It's my lethargy I'm trying to kick. Give these people a break, Fischer, and listen to yourself!*

This is why those who judge will be judged: "For in the same way you judge others, you will be judged, and with the measure you use, it will be measured to you" (Matthew 7:2). It comes back like a boomerang. It stands to reason. I can only see in someone else what I am aware of in myself. This is not rocket science. I'm simply not smart enough to see anything other than what I know. It's a point of identification. This truth is so reliable that you can count on it for your own assessment. Identify the things that bother you most about other people and you'll have a pretty good idea where your own problems lie.

## Nothing for the man who has everything

No one is better at this than the Pharisee. Pharisees are impervious to truth. They are hardheaded; nothing gets in. Yet they render judgments on others all the time.

The Pharisees were a long way from applying the teachings of Jesus to their lives. They never even heard Jesus. Never gave him a chance. They were already experts on every possible avenue of religion and spirituality . . . why should they need to listen to another teacher? They had a system and they had it down.

Jesus wasn't some new teacher to investigate, bearing some new truth to contemplate; he was a threat to their authority. If they had been committed to truth they could have heard him out, but from the start they were committed only to *their* truth and on that they had the final word. This is one of the gravest dangers of a pharisaical position: it puts you above learning. When it came to religion, the Pharisees already knew everything there was to know, and what can you possibly give someone who has everything?

So instead of hearing what Jesus had to say, the Pharisees were only listening to prove him wrong. They were listening for a flaw, a crack in the wall, a weakness to exploit. They never asked a question to find the answer; they asked their questions to trap Jesus and hopefully show him up. As far as they were concerned, Jesus was an itinerant preacher with a dangerously high level of charisma who was capable of taking the people away from them. Their job was to catch him in a snare—to show the people he was going against the laws of Moses. Questions like "Is there truth in what he's saying? Could this be for me?" weren't permitted to nest in their minds precisely because their minds were already made up.

## You'll wonder where the wonder went

Pharisees never apply anything to themselves because they are already experts on everything. An expert has ceased the process of learning and has turned from a disciple into a critic—from a learner into a spurner. It can happen to any Christian, and at some time in our Christian walk, I believe it happens to us all. This is why a little knowledge is a dangerous thing. Pharisees know just enough to think they know it all. If they knew just a little bit more, they would realize how much they don't know.

"The man who thinks he knows something does not yet know as he ought to know," says Paul (1 Corinthians 8:2). Paul once knew just enough about Jesus to judge him as an impostor and persecute his followers. He was not doing this just to be mean. He was sincerely protecting what he thought was the truth. It took a blinding light on Damascus Road to show him how blind he really was about Jesus, and how much he had to learn.

There is no greater obstacle to truth and revelation than to think you already know what you need to know. This attitude is usually accompanied by a critical spirit. We are quick to apply teaching and rebuke to others since we clearly do not need it ourselves.

This happens to all of us at some point. The newness wears off, the joy of discovery dies in the supposed knowing of everything we need to know, and the childlike wonder slowly slips into a cynicism that makes us old before our time. It's a gradual thing—too gradual usually to notice.

I first experienced this cynicism when I went away to a Christian college, and I see it at work today in similar Christian environments. Cynicism is a dangerous spiritual virus that grows in the Petri dish of familiarity. It's hard to keep a vital faith when everyone you know is a Christian. No one has to articulate the faith in a context in which it is assumed, and if we don't have to articulate our faith or meet daily challenges to it, then we don't grow. We assume we know a lot more than we do until soon we are sporting all the vital ingredients for a healthy Pharisee—superior knowledge, imperviousness to truth, and a critical spirit.

This is when we start applying truth to everyone but ourselves. We see what's wrong with everything. We become impatient, old, hard-headed, and sarcastic. We can't understand how everyone else can be so dumb. When Paul speaks about the Jews in the book of Romans, he has this attitude pegged. He also has his finger on the cause of the problem.

> Now you, if you call yourself a Jew; if you rely on the law and brag about your relationship to God; if you know his will and approve of what is superior because you are instructed by the law; if you are convinced that you are a guide for the blind, a light for those who are in the dark, an instructor of the foolish, a teacher of infants, because you have in the law the embodiment of knowledge and truth—you, then, who teach others, do you not teach yourself? (Romans 2:17–21)

The last five words should scream at us about now. *Do you not teach yourself?* When it comes to spiritual things, no teacher can be above being taught. The words we apply to others must be first applied to us. It is the only way to keep from becoming a Pharisee. Just as we judge what we are guilty of ourselves, so we teach what we need. Never from a superior place, but from a place where the truth has first touched our lives and brought us to our knees.

## Old dogs; new tricks

"The man who thinks he knows something does not yet know as he ought to know" (1 Corinthians 8:2). Look at this verse again. It implies that when we know as we ought to know, we will be conscious of our own ignorance. That is an important aspect of knowledge the Pharisees missed. There is a humility that comes with true knowledge. In some ways it's like starting over. We see that what we thought we knew, we didn't really know after all. This is liberating in that it brings back that childlike wonder we once knew.

Ever been around new believers? They are wide-eyed with amazement. They lap up everything they can get. They feel like they have such a long way to go, but they are happy to be on the right road, nonetheless. There is an innocence to their learning and yearning. It would be unthinkable for them to apply a teaching to anyone but themselves because a new believer assumes everybody else knows more than they do. They are the antithesis to the Pharisees in every way.

Put yourself in the place of a new believer. No matter how long you have been a Christian, the last few sentences can still be true about you. Read them again in your mind. *I am wide-eyed with amazement. I lap up everything I can get. I feel like I have such a long way to go, but I am happy to be on the right road, nonetheless. There is an innocence to my learning and yearning. It would be unthinkable for me to apply a teaching to anyone but myself because I assume everybody else knows more than I do.*

Old believers should always feel new. The way out for us Pharisees is to take everything we know and apply it to ourselves and, as part of our recovery, leave everyone else to the Lord. Paul would say, "Teach yourself." If the Pharisees had done this, they would have recognized Jesus as being from God.

Faith is always new. Only children get into the kingdom of heaven.

"Old" is not a part of the vocabulary of faith. Learning, growing, yearning for more, seeing things from other perspectives—this is how we stay young in faith. The definition of a disciple is a learner, and there is no evidence that the disciples ever ceased being disciples. Once a learner, always a learner. Read the New Testament and substitute "learners" for "disciples" and you might more readily find yourself among them. These were not spiritual giants; like us, they were people in process. Here are some examples:

"If you hold to my teaching, you are really my [learners]" (John 8:31).

"By this all men will know that you are my [learners], if you love one another" (John 13:35).

"This is to my Father's glory, that you bear much fruit, showing yourselves to be my [learners]" (John 15:8).

"So the word of God spread. The number of [learners] in Jerusalem increased rapidly" (Acts 6:7).

"And the [learners] were filled with joy and with the Holy Spirit" (Acts 13:52).

"Then they returned to Lystra, Iconium and Antioch, strengthening the [learners] and encouraging them to remain true to the faith" (Acts 14:21–22).

*Learners.* I can be one of them. You can too. Forget about everybody else and follow Jesus. Peter had to learn this lesson through one last rebuke from Jesus, and this after being forgiven for his denial and reunited with the risen Christ.

Jesus was walking along with Peter and some of the others in their last recorded moments together on earth. Christ had just prophesied concerning the manner in which Peter would die and glorify God, when Peter noticed John following them and his foot went right into his mouth again: "Lord, what about him?"

To which Jesus replied, "If I want him to remain alive until I return, what is that to you? You must follow me" (John 21:21–22). *Ouch!* In this somewhat caustic retort, Jesus revealed an important truth we need to know about avoiding the pitfalls of the Pharisees. How God works with other people is his business, not mine. My business is to follow him.

There is great liberty in this. It is a letting go. A coming down off the pedestal of pride. Let's face it, it's a heavy burden being a Pharisee: managing truth, defending God, stalking heresy, enforcing the rules, and keeping those out of the kingdom who do not belong there. I wouldn't wish being responsible for everybody else on anyone. No wonder the Pharisees were such an unhappy lot! Long faces, long robes, long ledgers, long lists. It's enough to make you tired just thinking about it. What a relief to let go of all this and simply follow Christ!

"Come to me, all you who are weary and burdened, and I will give you rest. Take my yoke upon you and learn from me, for I am gentle and humble in heart, and you will find rest for your souls" (Matthew 11:28–29). How could we learn from someone gentle and humble in heart and not end up the same way?

## What's in it for me?

My soul yearns for you in the night; in the morning my spirit longs for you. When your judgments come upon the earth, the people of the world learn righteousness. (Isaiah 26:9–10)

I cry a lot at church now. More than I ever remember. I am fortunate to attend a church full of broken people with a compassionate, understanding pastor who encourages us through his own struggles. He doesn't seem like the pastor type; he's much too shy. My wife leans over to me when he gets up to preach and whispers, "He's so brave." You sense he is overcoming many internal barriers just to get up there. And when he speaks, he reminds us of his humanity, and thus, our own.

I love the benediction most of all. It's never the same. It's always tied to what we learned that morning, but it is always full of Christ's provision to live in us and accomplish all these new things we have just become aware of that can seem so overwhelming. Our pastor always lifts his hands for this part and I am certain someone or something covers me in that moment. God's presence in me is affirmed and called out and I feel his embrace. I need this. I need to know he is here with me. Life is difficult. Sometimes I feel alone even with his Spirit in me.

I get real selfish at church now; I say to myself: "What's in this for me?" But I think I have it right. What I mean is: "How does this apply to me? Not anybody else. I'm the one he's speaking to. I'm the one this message is designed for." I never get excused around truth because there's always more for me to learn. I'm a learner. This is what I do. I learn from the teacher; I learn from those around me; I learn from someone else's perspective; I come to church to learn.

I have to fight it, though. The temptation to listen on someone else's behalf is huge, especially if my kids are there. I'm always listening for my son or my daughter, but they don't need my help. They will get what they are supposed to get. They will probably teach *me* from what they got. Jesus would say to me: *What is that to you? You must follow me.*

## How can a man be born when he is old?

Is it any wonder that in the one recorded account of Jesus with a Pharisee who was vulnerable enough to at least go to him and ask him some real questions, Jesus immediately began talking about the need to be a learner all over again?

He went to Jesus under a cloak of darkness. He had seen Jesus perform signs that, in his opinion, only someone from God could do, and he wanted to know: Was he really from God? Old Nicodemus had a crack in his all-knowing armor.

Jesus did not answer his question directly. Before Nicodemus could understand anything about Christ he would have to see and understand the kingdom of God. And before he could see and understand the kingdom of God he would have to experience another kind of birth. And so the first thing Jesus said to him, almost as if he didn't hear the question, was: "I tell you the truth, no one can see the kingdom of God unless he is born again" (John 3:3).

Nicodemus's response to this demand is rife with irony. "How can a man be born when he is old?"

That is the paramount question for any Pharisee. How can you be born when you are old? How can you be ignorant when you know so much? How can you become a child when you are an adult? How can a teacher become a learner? How can those enmeshed as deeply as Pharisees are in a system of religious piety admit that what they've been doing is not leading people to God after all? How do blind guides admit they are blind? How can a wealthy, powerful, respected Pharisee like Nicodemus accept that a poor itinerant (some say illegitimate) preacher who came from God-knows-where is the master and Lord of all? How can this Pharisee bow down and worship a peasant? Can he bend that far? How does someone in his position do that? How does a Pharisee start over again?

"How can a man be born when he is old?"

Nicodemus is going to have to answer this question in order to shed this heavy cloak.

What follows in Jesus' answer to this question is his most eloquent statement of the gospel, including the famous John 3:16: "For God so loved the world that he gave his one and only Son, that whoever believes in him shall not perish but have eternal life."

This is where those of us who have become modern-day evangelical Pharisees differ from the original Jewish Pharisees. We have the answer to our self-righteousness embedded in our own message. The Pharisees had the law and the customs as part of their tradition. They had to break with their past in order to accept Jesus. We have only to embrace our past and our tradition, for the Christian church is strewn with forgiven sinners who have found glorious absolution in Christ.

We have the answer; we've had it for two thousand years. It's the most important part of our ritual and our liturgy. We sing the answer and preach the answer and even share the answer with others who haven't heard. We partake of the answer from a shared table. All we have to do is simply apply the answer to ourselves. We are the ones Christ died for; we are the ones who need to be born again. We are the ones who need to join the ranks of the multitudes of sinners who have found forgiveness at the foot of the cross. We need to remember who we are and how we got in and who our new friends are now that we are here.

*I used to think that I was right,*
*A lonely candle in the night.*
*And while the heart of the world was breaking*
*I could not feel the aching.*
*The mantle had passed down to me,*
*This thing was my destiny.*
*But while the world was out there dying*
*I was in here lying to myself.*
*For all the knowledge I had gained*
*Put me on a higher plane,*
*And I became another.*
*No one was my brother,*
*And the loving message He brought down*
*Turned into a hollow sound.*
*And then I heard Him calling,*
*And His words sent me falling to my knees.*
*And suddenly there was with me*
*An ocean of humanity,*
*A sea of many faces*
*In waves of warm embraces.*
*And while I questioned how to judge them all,*
*Who would rise and who would fall,*
*I found myself among them,*
*And it mattered little who was wrong or right.*
*And then I saw Him lifted up,*
*The wounded one who drank the cup*
*Of death for all the dying,*
*The end of justifying.*
*And I laid my mantle on the ground*
*And felt the rain come pouring down.*
*The rain of my religion*
*Falling down like weeping from the sky.*
—from the song "The Only One" by John Fischer

The answer to Pharisaism is to be born again. It's the same answer Nicodemus received. "For God did not send his Son into the world to condemn the world, but to save the world through him" (John 3:17). The answer is salvation—our salvation and the salvation of countless others. The answer is the gospel. We've already got our answer; we have only to remind ourselves of it and embrace it personally each day.

*Step 1* We admit that our single most unmitigated pleasure is to judge other people.

*Step 2* Have come to believe that our means of obtaining greatness is to make everyone lower than ourselves in our own mind.

*Step 3* Realize that we detest mercy being given to those who, unlike us, haven't worked for it and don't deserve it.

*Step 4* Have decided that we don't want to get what we deserve after all, and we don't want anyone else to either.

*Step 5* Will cease all attempts to apply teaching and rebuke to anyone but ourselves.

*Step 6* Are ready to have God remove all these defects of attitude and character.

*Step 7* Embrace the belief that we are, and will always be, experts at sinning.

*Step 8* Are looking closely at the lives of famous men and women of the Bible who turned out to be ordinary sinners like us.

*Step 9* Are seeking through prayer and meditation to make a conscious effort to consider others better than ourselves.

*Step 10* Embrace the state of astonishment as a permanent and glorious reality.

*Step 11* Choose to rid ourselves of any attitude that is not bathed in gratitude.

*Step 12* Having had a spiritual awakening as the result of these steps, we will try to carry this message to others who think that Christians are better than everyone else.

# STEP 6

*We are ready to have God remove all these defects of attitude and character.*

> Before we can be greatly used by God
> we must see the monstrous evil
> in our souls.
>
> DAVID ROPER

NOW FOR THE HARD PART, THE SHEDDING OF THIS MANTLE—THIS cloak of self-righteousness and definable spirituality that has secured our place in the spiritual order of things. Unlike a coat that can be easily removed, this mantle is more like a second skin.

In the beloved *Chronicles of Narnia* by C. S. Lewis, Eustace develops a thick dragonlike skin that he cannot shed. He has to go through a number of steps to lose this skin, the last being its painful tearing away. This pharisaical cloak we wear does not come off very easily.

## Second-generation Pharisee

There is no one more capable of relating this process to us than the apostle Paul, formerly Saul of Tarsus. His way of life and his identity were stripped from him when he chose to follow Christ and answer God's call to be an apostle to the Gentiles. He lost everything in the process, including his name.

Paul made good use of his pharisaical roots, however, even after his conversion. Upon his arrest in Jerusalem, he called upon this tradition by claiming he was not only a Pharisee but a second-generation Pharisee. "I am a Pharisee, the son of a Pharisee" (Acts 23:6).

Just what were the Pharisees like in Paul's day? They were the ones in charge of writing down and interpreting the law. In the second century B.C. they were called Hasidaeans or "God's loyal ones." Jesus often spoke of "the scribes and Pharisees" in the same breath because both groups were carrying on the tradition of the scribes of Old Testament times, the ones who literally "got it all down." They were the spiritual descendants of Ezra, writing and copying the Word of God and responsible for interpreting it to the people. Sometimes they did this to their own advantage. For instance, they established the contents of the written Torah by determining 613 commandments and interpreting and supplementing them so that there would be no possibility of a Pharisee breaking a law by accident or by ignorance. It was by this means that they were able to claim total ethical righteousness. This was the process Paul referred to that allowed him (as Saul) to consider himself faultless as to legalistic righteousness (Philippians 3:6).

Righteousness for the Pharisees was a system, not an inner reality. It was external, not internal. It was, from beginning to end, a calculated manipulation of the law that awarded them technical righteousness, albeit through a cold heart.

Everything the Pharisees did revolved around the law. They tracked their authority all the way back to Moses on Sinai, and blamed the Babylonian Exile on the failure of Israel to keep the Torah. Because their rigorous interpretation of the Torah had little intrinsic appeal to common people, they were guaranteed a minority status. They could consider themselves "separate ones," not only in charge of the law but in their minds following it to perfection. Even today this is a powerful position to hold and an addiction not easily shaken. Being in control of the rules by which you pass yourself and fail almost everyone else is indeed heady stuff.

Thus it was not an easy thing for Saul to give up his status. It took nothing short of a personal miraculous encounter with God and a helpless blindness to strip away his thick-skinned righteousness. Is it any wonder that Saul's return to sight was described as "something like scales" falling from his eyes? (Acts 9:18). Eustace would have understood.

## In his own words

There is no better way to learn from Paul's story than to hear it out of his own mouth. When he was in Jerusalem about to be seized by a rioting mob incited by the Jewish leaders, he claimed protection as a Roman citizen and under that protection obtained permission to address the crowd. Here, then, is his story.

"I am a Jew, born in Tarsus of Cilicia, but brought up in this city. Under Gamaliel I was thoroughly trained in the law of our fathers and was just as zealous for God as any of you are today. I persecuted the followers of this Way to their death, arresting both men and women and throwing them into prison, as also the high priest and all the Council can testify. I even obtained letters from them to their brothers in Damascus, and went there to bring these people as prisoners to Jerusalem to be punished.

"About noon as I came near Damascus, suddenly a bright light from heaven flashed around me. I fell to the ground and heard a voice say to me, 'Saul! Saul! Why do you persecute me?'

" 'Who are you, Lord?' I asked.

" 'I am Jesus of Nazareth, whom you are persecuting,' he replied. My companions saw the light, but they did not understand the voice of him who was speaking to me.

" 'What shall I do, Lord?' I asked.

" 'Get up,' the Lord said, 'and go into Damascus. There you will be told all that you have been assigned to do.' My companions led me by the hand into Damascus, because the brilliance of the light had blinded me.

"A man named Ananias came to see me. He was a devout observer of the law and highly respected by all the Jews living there. He stood beside me and said, 'Brother Saul, receive your sight!' And at that very moment I was able to see him.

"Then he said: 'The God of our fathers has chosen you to know his will and to see the Righteous One and to hear words from his mouth. You will be his witness to all men of what you have seen and heard. And now what are you waiting for? Get up, be baptized and wash your sins away, calling on his name'" (Acts 22:3–16).

## The reeducation of Saul of Tarsus

There are a number of things in this story, as Paul tells it, that are indicative of the process of shedding one's pharisaical skin in any age or time, the first and most obvious being a direct encounter with the almighty God. It is a terrifying and humbling thing for a so-called expert on God to actually meet up with him. All pious words turn to chalk in the mouth. Even worse if the position of power as God's representative was used in a manipulative way to control or lord it over people. Suddenly the gig is up. You are on your knees before the real God and you have nothing to say for yourself.

"Saul! Saul! Why do you persecute me?" cut through all of Saul's righteous indignation and pharisaical pride. Here was Saul, supposedly defending the truth from an onslaught of blasphemy, and suddenly God is equating himself with the very people Saul was trying to silence. Not good news for Saul, but it was the truth. The removal of defects in attitude and character always begins by an encounter with the painful truth—the truth about God and us and how we are wrong.

The correct human response to this is usually the same. "I fell to the ground," Paul said, and this typifies a new humility forced upon someone by the truth. When anyone has an encounter with God it is like this. The end result will be a new empowerment to do God's will, but that comes only through the realization that you have *not* been doing God's will heretofore. You have actually been working against him.

This is one of the hardest things for Pharisees to face. Acting supposedly on God's behalf as "God's loyal ones," they were, nonetheless, working against him. Pharisees rely on human effort and control to accomplish God's work in the world. It may be a noble task undertaken by noble people, but it is flawed in spite of all its good intentions. Its fatal error is that God wants to work his will in and through humble people rather than to have prideful people doing what they think is right.

God wanted Saul to stop his defense of the Jewish laws and traditions of his day and sit down and shut up and wait for instructions from the Holy Spirit. His work for God was becoming a hindrance to God's larger work that was already under way. It would take a complete reeducation of Saul to adjust to God's way, and, in Saul's case, that turned out to be a fourteen-year process (Galatians 1:17; 2:1).

Thus Saul not only encountered God, he began a lengthy process of learning from God afresh. Old ways are hard to change. Leaders have to become students. Guides must learn to follow. Scales must fall off. Thick skin must be shed.

## The blind leading the blind

In Saul's place, this humility was graphically illustrated through his temporary blindness. First, it put him in a completely helpless state: imagine Saul, the protector and defender of the Torah—the persecutor of all who fail to see—suddenly needing to be led around by his traveling companions because he couldn't see where to take the next step. This is the man who struck fear in the hearts of the early church—who went to Damascus with a list of Christians to root out and punish—groping around in his own personal darkness.

It was God's irony to put Saul through this particular physical ordeal as a symbol of his own spiritual blindness. Over and over Jesus accused the Pharisees of being blind guides and blind fools leading others into their own error. "If a blind man leads a blind man, both will fall into a pit" (Matthew 15:14). Suddenly, Saul was forced to experience the physical reality of his true spiritual condition. He was blind. He did not know where he was going.

He was also forced to have to trust someone else to lead him for a change—someone he might have formerly judged as being beneath him.

It is often an exercise in small group dynamics to take turns at being blindfolded and led around by someone else. It is a scary and humiliating experience and one that teaches total trust, even in someone who might not be considered trustworthy.

Pharisees generally are not very trusting. They are suspicious of everyone, and as we found out in Step 2, they put themselves over everyone so that they are never in a place of depending on anyone but themselves. To have to be suddenly dependent on someone who you thought of as inferior to you is a true lesson in humility and a lesson in trusting God. Leaders have a hard time being led.

These steps, or something close to them, are what we can expect to have happen to us in some form if we are to recover from our pharisaical blindness. This is usually how God works. He puts us in a humiliating state that nothing short of his intervention can redeem. But herein lies also his mercy, for in being healed, we experience the confirming miracle of God.

If Saul had any doubts about the validity of his miraculous experience on Damascus Road, they would have all been dispelled when a certain Jewish stranger by the name of Ananias came to him and prayed, and immediately his sight returned. The blindness was humiliating; the healing was sweet. Saul was now ready to listen. His pride and haughtiness had fallen along with the scales from his eyes. His blindness was taken away. He was now stripped of anything he could take credit for and was humbly ready for God's instructions. And what was his first assignment? "Get up, be baptized and wash your sins away, calling on his name."

## What sins?

Telling a Pharisee to go wash his sins away is a contradiction in terms. What sins? We've already seen how Pharisees in Saul's day were faultless in their own eyes. That Saul could even consider himself a sinner in need of repentance showed great awareness and a sudden change of heart. The heart had been softened and convicted. It had faced the real guilt inside through a blinding encounter with God on the road and three days of total darkness. We can only speculate on the things

Saul saw in the dark, but much of it must have had to do with his sinfulness.

Jesus seemed ready to move Saul right along on this program of recovery. Telling him to go wash his sins away assumed he had become aware of them, and from the continuation of his story, we can tell he had.

> "When I returned to Jerusalem and was praying at the temple, I fell into a trance and saw the Lord speaking. 'Quick!' he said to me. 'Leave Jerusalem immediately, because they will not accept your testimony about me.'
>
> " 'Lord,' I replied, 'these men know that I went from one synagogue to another to imprison and beat those who believe in you. And when the blood of your martyr Stephen was shed, I stood there giving my approval and guarding the clothes of those who were killing him' " (Acts 22:17–20).

One of the devastating revelations that came to Saul when the scales fell from his eyes was the fact that he had indeed been persecuting God. In the name of everything he thought was right, he had been beating up on innocent people and imprisoning them for fabricated crimes. The entire system of the Pharisees was fabricated. And it had taken Saul this long—all the way to the stoning of Stephen, whom Paul calls in his speech the Lord's martyr—to see it. Paul was admitting to a murder. The robes at his feet were a sign of responsibility. This realization deeply affected him in a way that he never got over.

But Saul had other sins to wash away as well. Certainly persecuting—even killing—innocent people would be high on the list. Spiritual pride was probably another. Then there had to be some inner secret sins that haunted him. We know this inner inconsistency was common to all Pharisees or someone would have thrown stones at the prostitute in John's account ("If any one of you is without sin, let him be the first to throw a stone at her," John 8:7). The fact that no one did proved that they all harbored sin in their hearts and knew it. They all had their own private brand of sin that turned them daily into hypocrites. Saul, when told to wash his sins away, showed no objection. He knew what they were and he was ready to get rid of them. And so "he got up and was baptized, and after taking some food, he regained his strength" (Acts 9:18–19).

## Down to the water

Like blindness, baptism is also humbling. There is something about going down in the water and relying on someone else to lift you up that is impossible to do while still holding on to pride and arrogance. It signifies an abandonment to God that has already begun. And like the blindfold routine, it requires a great deal of trust. You cross your arms over your chest and lean back into whoever is holding you. Totally at the other's mercy, you go down. For a moment you are underwater, separated from the oxygen of human life as a symbol of dying to self, and then lifted up out of the water in newness of life, cleansed from your sins by the blood of Jesus. For a Pharisee, this experience would be completely foreign and virtually impossible to go through without a formidable change of heart. Remember, these are the guys who like to control everything spiritual.

But Saul did not seem to have any trouble with this either. Whatever he saw about himself in those three days of darkness was enough to humble him and make him ready to surrender. I'm sure that when he went down into that water, his sins were known to him, and when he came up, they were miraculously lifted from his soul. It's the same kind of liberation that happens to everyone who has ever been baptized into Christ. "My sins were washed away, and my night was turned to day. Heaven came down and glory filled my soul."

## The submission of suffering

When Ananias first received the assignment from God to go to Saul and pray for him, he balked, knowing Saul's reputation as a persecutor of God's saints in Jerusalem. To which the Lord replied, "Go! This man is my chosen instrument to carry my name before the Gentiles and their kings and before the people of Israel. I will show him how much he must suffer for my name" (Acts 9:15–16).

This is the final instrument God uses to tear away our pharisaical scales. It is the one that will stay with us on this journey as a constant reminder. Blindness and baptism had to do with Saul's conversion— God used them to turn him dramatically around—but suffering is the way he kept Paul humble and dependent on him. It is the same for us. Suffering is also that which purges us of recurring pharisaical habits and attitudes. "I will show him how much he must suffer for my name" makes God look almost masochistic here, except that he knows what purpose the suffering will play in the life of Paul. Remember, this prediction of suffering is how God answered Ananias's initial fear of Saul. The implication is that suffering will smooth the sharp edges; it will turn Saul into a compassionate Paul. *Don't worry, Ananias,* it seems God was saying, *this man who has persecuted so many will now receive, in full measure, what he has been dishing out, and it will make him a different person. He is about to suffer alongside those he has been persecuting. He is not to be feared, for the submission of suffering will soften his heart and make him your friend.*

We know from the rest of this story that the suffering of Paul took on many different forms. Physical hardship, abandonment, disappointment, and even a chronic "thorn in the flesh" all played a part in Paul's growth. We need to accept that there are some weaknesses God leaves as a reminder, lest the pride return and we think that by our own righteousness we have gotten our victories.

## The Pharisee's statement of profit and loss

From the helplessness of blindness, to the humility of baptism, to the submission of suffering, Saul the Pharisee was being broken and remade into Paul, the great apostle of the church. The process he went through is not that different from what any recovering Pharisee will face in shedding that familiar dragon skin of self-righteousness. The same basic errors have been made; the same perspectives have been skewed. A new identity must be formed; a new trust built. All in all, it's a new point of reference—one that caused Paul to write:

If anyone else thinks he has reasons to put confidence in the flesh, I have more: circumcised on the eighth day, of the people of Israel, of the tribe of Benjamin, a Hebrew of Hebrews; in regard to the law, a Pharisee; as for zeal, persecuting the church; as for legalistic righteousness, faultless.

But whatever was to my profit I now consider loss for the sake of Christ. What is more, I consider everything a loss compared to the surpassing greatness of knowing Christ Jesus my Lord, for whose sake I have lost all things. I consider them rubbish, that I may gain Christ and be found in him, not having a righteousness of my own that comes from the law, but that which is through faith in Christ—the righteousness that comes from God and is by faith. (Philippians 3:4–9)

I have had a number of knowledgeable students of biblical Greek point out to me that the word translated here "rubbish" is a mild rendering of a colloquial word Paul chose to use that, more accurately translated, would be unprintable in a book by this publisher. Perhaps it could read, "I consider them [expletive deleted], that I may gain Christ. . . ."

It is remarkable that Paul would show such distaste for these things, none of which are bad in and of themselves. His circumcision, his Jewish roots, his commitment to the law, his zeal—all are admirable. Why would he make such a harsh statement? Why does he hate these things so much? It must be that he hated the role they played in his life. He hated them not for their intrinsic value or lack of it, but for how he used them. They were never intended to provide what he tried to receive from them, and what he did receive turned out to be false.

Paul's background, his zeal, and his legalistic righteousness were essential to maintaining the false identity of Saul of Tarsus. They were the means by which he assessed himself and judged others. They were a source of spiritual pride that only drove him further away from God and away from other people. They even disqualified him for the cross since Christ died only for sinners. These were the things that turned Saul into a very lonely, angry man who was on a mission to persecute anyone who was free and happy in Christ.

The problem was he drew something from these things. They were a profit to him, like a spiritual investment in some pseudo-spiritual bank account that paid ill-gotten dividends of worth, power, and prestige. Once Paul experienced real worth, value, and identity in Christ he no longer wanted to have anything to do with the former things. In fact, he was willing to take all his pharisaical assets and throw them on the refuse pile, because he knew, in the end, that they had profited him nothing.

Every recovering Pharisee can make her own list of human assets that, like Paul's list, keep her from knowing Christ. These are the natural things we trust in. These are actually our strengths—our talent, our background, our good record, our spiritual status, even our noble stand against sin. These are the things we hold on to that make us different and separate us from the crowd. These are the things that we think make us worthy to be Christians. What would Paul say about these things? As they say in England, "Down the loo." Put this stuff where it belongs and flush it.

Now we are getting to the heart of the matter. The liabilities of the Pharisees do not reside in weaknesses, but in the things in which they are naturally strong. This is what Paul meant by putting confidence in the flesh. He merely listed his natural assets, and as Pharisees go, he's got us all beat. We, then, should pay close attention to his comment that these things were not worth the paper they were written on.

For a recovering Pharisee, natural assets are like an alcoholic's drink. They are what we have relied upon for so long and what we are afraid to do without. We feel naked without one of these in hand. We go to a party and have to have one served up right away.

When we are afraid or feel vulnerable, we fall back on a talent or a natural skill that we can trust in to be there for us. And yet all of these things, as good as they may be, keep us from Christ.

To know Christ is to be vulnerable, to renounce any dependency apart from him, to stand there without a drink in your hand and look forward to a sober day in his company, to be without any personal assets but Christ alone. This is the goal of every recovering Pharisee and every Christian. If you truly want to know God, then get ready to be stripped of all you thought you had.

It's the Pharisee's statement of profit and loss: My profit is my loss; my loss is my gain.

*Step 1* We admit that our single most unmitigated pleasure is to judge other people.

*Step 2* Have come to believe that our means of obtaining greatness is to make everyone lower than ourselves in our own mind.

*Step 3* Realize that we detest mercy being given to those who, unlike us, haven't worked for it and don't deserve it.

*Step 4* Have decided that we don't want to get what we deserve after all, and we don't want anyone else to either.

*Step 5* Will cease all attempts to apply teaching and rebuke to any-one but ourselves.

*Step 6* Are ready to have God remove all these defects of attitude and character.

*Step 7* Embrace the belief that we are, and will always be, experts at sinning.

*Step 8* Are looking closely at the lives of famous men and women of the Bible who turned out to be ordinary sinners like us.

*Step 9* Are seeking through prayer and meditation to make a con-scious effort to consider others better than ourselves.

*Step 10* Embrace the state of astonishment as a permanent and glorious reality.

*Step 11* Choose to rid ourselves of any attitude that is not bathed in gratitude.

*Step 12* Having had a spiritual awakening as the result of these steps, we will try to carry this message to others who think that Christians are better than everyone else.

# *We embrace the belief that we are, and will always be, experts at sinning.*

> [Sin] is my nature, the only thing I know
> how to do.
>
> B R O T H E R   L A W R E N C E

---

I N THE COURSE OF ONE PRIVATE CONVERSATION BETWEEN THE TWO of them, my mother informed my wife that I didn't sin. Now, my wife had been married to me for over ten years at the time, and, as you can imagine, she had a somewhat differing opinion on the subject of my sinfulness or lack of it. I was pretty shocked myself to hear of my supposed perfection, and though I would love to believe my mother, I'm afraid my wife knows better. Though we often joke about this now, I wonder what would bring my mother to pose such a preposterous claim about me. Aside from the expected parental my-son-can-do-no-wrong myth, was there anything more indicated in this dubious assessment? I believe that there might have been.

Many evangelicals mistakenly believe that a person's spirituality and closeness to God are inversely proportionate to the amount of sin in that person's life. More sin, less of God; more of God, less sin, the ultimate goal being sinlessness—a state that no one we know has actually achieved, but is theoretically plausible nonetheless. I guess my mother had me so close to God that I had to be sinless in her mind.

This equation is carefully bolstered by glowing testimonies and the close-to-perfect reputations of those who are close to God. Ministers and those in "full-time Christian service" are closer than anybody and thus the furthest from sin. This is why it is so devastating to the church when these close-to-perfect people fall prey to a terrible moral failure. The result is shock and disbelief. They were so spiritual; how could this have happened?

## The big Christian lie

In his charming coming-of-age novel, *Portofino*, Frank Schaeffer, son of Francis and Edith Schaeffer, two of the most important Christian thinkers in the last three decades, strips the veneer away from what many must have thought was the ideal Christian family.

Frank—formerly Franky—paints a picture in this novel of a fundamentalist evangelical family on vacation in Italy over the course of two summers. The parallels between the story and what I know about Frank's own family and childhood are everywhere. In the story we see a distant, silent father, who in public is fighting for a culturally relevant biblical orthodoxy but in private is prone to huge mood swings and a violent temper, a wife who fights with him over which one of them is more spiritual, and children who are forced to be "biblical" before they know what any of it means. Though some of the situations are humorous and charming, others are too painfully real to just be funny. Having grown up in a similar evangelical family caught in a public and private dichotomy, I find *Portofino* cathartic, to say the least.

In looking into this story, I discovered that I have two reactions to this dysfunctional Christian family. The first is to take some pleasure in their shortcomings because then I can feel somehow better about mine. The second reaction is to be disappointed. Something inside me wishes Frank hadn't uncovered this flawed family portrait because then I could go on believing that at least someone I revered, like Francis and Edith Schaeffer, had gotten it right.

It occurs to me that this second reaction could be thought of as the big Christian lie. That is, the belief that somebody, somewhere, got it right. Don't we flock to speakers and singers who are up front and important because they are getting it right, and aren't they up there because we expect that of them? When it becomes painfully obvious that in some area of their lives they did not get it right, aren't they promptly removed from their place? Aren't all those smiling people on the covers of Christian books telling us how we, too, can get it right if we follow their advice? If we didn't worship at the altar of getting it right, there wouldn't be a market for half this stuff.

But have no fear, Christian entrepreneurs, the market is not in any danger, because this appeal has held human beings in its grip ever since Moses came down the mountain with God's top ten list for getting it right. And we all carry on with the lie.

## The lure of the "almost"

Unfortunately, getting it right is not the issue. If we were all facing sin more realistically, we would not be so surprised when it shows up in the life of a spiritual leader. (I sometimes fear what my children will write about me!) If we were being truthful about who we really are—all of us—we would know that our leaders are human, just as we are.

Sometimes I wonder if we want our spiritual leaders to be perfect so we don't have to be. As long as we believe somebody's perfect, we can go on perpetuating the myth that perfection is possible and keep on shrouding our own sin safely behind the lie of the "almost." We are *almost* there. We have *almost* arrived. We are *almost* holy. One more book, one more seminar, one more revival service, and we will be just like the person on the cover of the book or the brochure. That's why when leaders fall, it blows the cover on this charade. Suddenly this elusive spiritual life we are trying to lead is further away than we thought. "Almost" is not even close. If the pastor can fall, what does that say about our chances?

If we were more honest with ourselves, we would know that the real question is not how someone so high could fall so far, but rather why hasn't it happened sooner in such an atmosphere of denial? What were these people doing up there in the first place; and what were we doing putting them there? The real problem in this case is not with sin, it is with our false idea of who we think we are. We need to understand that when someone falls, it's not the end; it's just the truth finally being known. It's actually a good thing if it sends us all back to the gospel, where we should have been all along.

I often wonder how a gospel based solely on the merits of one who has died to forgive sin could be perpetuated on the merits of those who don't seem to need it. If the whole point of the gospel is forgiveness of sin, then why do we insist on continually parading these *almost perfect* lives in front of each other? How has it happened that the people who proclaim forgiveness of sin don't seem to have any sins to be forgiven of themselves? How has a church that once was the happy possession of common fishermen and prostitutes and tax collectors become the home of the spiritually elite? There are, undoubtedly, numerous and complicated answers to these questions, but I believe at the root of them all is lurking the issue of the Pharisee.

## The call of the ancient Pharisee

Sin has a way of showing up only on the front end of salvation. Sinners are those who need to be saved, but once they are saved we rarely hear about sin anymore. Yes, sin still turns up in the context of all those sinners "out there" who need Jesus, but don't we "in here" need Jesus just as much after we're saved?

It's as if we believe another standard takes over once we become Christians. The unbeliever receives forgiveness of sins; the believer, however, must simply stop sinning. The blood of Jesus Christ covered my sin when I became a Christian, but now that I am saved I'd better straighten up and fly right. Salvation is for those who need to be saved, not those who already have been. And whenever *not sinning* takes precedence over *the forgiveness of sin* . . . beware the Pharisee.

"Who among you is without sin?" is the damning question Jesus posed to the Pharisees. We should ask ourselves the same question. John put it another way: "If we claim to be without sin, we deceive ourselves" (1 John 1:8). And yet we continue *to want* to be deceived—to perpetuate a myth about ourselves and our leaders that keeps our sin hidden from view because the alternative—to come clean—is just too scary. Although not sinning is not possible, we choose to perpetuate the false belief that it is, rather than face the truth. We created these perfect spiritual leaders in the first place to prove that it can be done; but they are living way beyond their spiritual means. If my assessment is true, it may actually be the grace of God that brings them down so we can all start facing the truth.

I grew up on hymn lyrics like, "What can wash away my sin? Nothing but the blood of Jesus." I notice the hymnist put this in the present tense, meaning that sin is a daily reality in the believer's life. But I have a hunch most people don't sing it that way. We sing it as if it were, "What has washed away my sin?" As if sin were now behind us— a remnant of our non-Christian past.

One can see how subtly we become prime candidates for the fraternity of Pharisees. When being perfect is more important than being saved—when not sinning takes precedence over honestly dealing with sin—all the same dynamics that tantalized Saul of Tarsus are waiting to empower us falsely. The supposed perfection, the arrangement of the standard so as to make the breaking of it almost impossible to do, the judgment of others, the hiding, and, of course, the hypocrisy, are simply too alluring to refuse.

## Foolish Galatians

"You foolish Galatians! Who has bewitched you?" wrote Paul in his letter to the same. "Are you so foolish? After beginning with the Spirit, are you now trying to attain your goal by human effort?" (Galatians 3:1, 3).

Apparently this is not a new problem. We start with the Spirit; we start with salvation; we start with the undeserved grace of God, but then human effort creeps back into our spiritual lives like weeds returning to a weeded garden. We start looking to ourselves again, thinking we have to come up with what we need to be good Christians, and the minute we start looking to ourselves, we start covering up and being defensive and comparing ourselves to others, just like Pharisees. It's inevitable: Where there is spirituality mixed with human effort, there will be all the pitfalls of the Pharisees, writhing like a brood of vipers waiting to entangle those who fall in.

If it took the Spirit to save us, Paul points out, it's going to take the Spirit to keep us saved. Start with the Spirit, *stay* with the Spirit; start with salvation, *stay* with salvation; start with grace, *stay* with grace. How can we add to what Christ has done? We are saved each day the same way we were saved the first time. We brought our sinful lives before God, turned from relying on ourselves to relying on him, and received his life in exchange for ours. It's no different now. It's a moment-by-moment transaction.

The Galatians were trying to perfect through human effort what the Spirit had begun without their help, while all along denying that very Spirit the right to their lives. Their problem was the same as the Pharisees: they wanted to be in control of the process. They wanted to take back what they gave up in the beginning. Apparently they were too uncomfortable not being in control. Who else would turn down the grace of God but someone who didn't want to be vulnerable to it? It's a tragedy that while there is grace to cover all our sin, there are still sinners who don't know about it and Pharisees who don't *want* to know.

## Salvation: then, now, and later

Confession of sin in our churches most often comes from those who are just being saved. We hear their stories as the equivalent of the "before" pictures in liposuction ads with all that detestable flab hanging out over the edges of ill-fitting bathing suits. The assumption is that the rest of us have had all the sin sucked out of our abs and buttocks and are currently enjoying our slim, trim "after" bodies. If sin does happen to show up later in a believer's life, it is the result of a temporary backsliding. It happens to the best of us now and then. This is "solved" by a simple rededication of our lives to God—a sort of "salvation refresher." Sin is rarely, if ever, addressed as a normal part of a believer's everyday experience.

Is salvation a one-time experience or something that we need every day of our lives? Yes and yes. These are actually two aspects of a three-pronged process of salvation—past, present, and future. The theological names for these three aspects of salvation are justification, sanctification, and glorification. Justification is what has happened to us in relation to our sin, once and for all, on the cross. Jesus Christ's death in our place has justified us forever before God and made possible our fellowship with him.

But this does not mean that we are sinless. Paul calls it a "body of death" that we still have to carry around in this life even though we have received the firstfruits of the Spirit in our hearts (Romans 8:23). We are currently caught between our ultimate glorification when we will receive our resurrection bodies like Christ, and the past-tense justification of ourselves through the finished work of Christ on the cross. Everything in between is our present-tense experience of the process of sanctification. That experience includes both sin and forgiveness of sin as a daily occurrence. Though our salvation is secured in heaven, we experience it currently as we struggle with our sin nature and feel God's knife cutting more deeply into the subtleties of our flesh.

The experience of sin in a believer's life is not always backsliding. Nor is it always willful disobedience. Often it is what is simply revealed or brought into view because of the Holy Spirit's work at peeling away our sin nature like the layers of an onion. The longer we follow Christ the more we discover how deep the sin goes and how deep and wide are his mercy and love. Realization of sin, confession, and forgiveness continue as we find out more about ourselves. This is why this process is both painful and rewarding. Painful because we keep discovering how far we still have to go, but rewarding because we keep discovering, as well, how far Christ has gone for us. This is also why the older believer always has an affinity for the new believer. It's the same process. The new believer may be experiencing God's forgiveness for the first time, but the experience is immediate, real, and necessary for both of them.

This is also why the new believer and the old believer can both sing the same song, tell the same gospel story, and talk of the same forgiveness fresh from each one's current experience of it. Take the following hymn:

> At the cross, at the cross, where I first saw the light,
> And the burden of my heart rolled away;
> It was there by faith I received my sight,
> And now I am happy all the day.

Does a twenty-year believer sing this song thinking back on twenty years ago when she received her forgiveness? Is the twenty-year believer remembering and vicariously experiencing her former forgiveness through the tears of the new convert? Or does the twenty-year believer have her own tears welling up in her eyes as she sings this hymn for the umpteenth time, realizing its implications even more deeply than the last time she sang it because of the sin for which she has just received fresh forgiveness? This is how our salvation continues to be alive in our lives.

"Tell Me the Old, Old Story" is another old hymn I remember singing often as a child. Well, the old, old story has a way of always being a new, new song when we understand and experience the painful and glorious process of our sanctification.

## More sin; more God

"The law was added so that the trespass might increase. But where sin increased, grace increased all the more" (Romans 5:20).

At the beginning of this chapter I talked about this erroneous equation: More sin, less of God; more of God, less sin. I would like to suggest at this point a different equation. I would like to suggest that more of God in my life actually means more sin, if by more sin it is clear I mean the *awareness* of sin. The person who is closer to God is more aware of sin than the one who is distant, and thus that person will be having a more relevant experience with God as he or she grows in the faith.

This is why older Christians keep getting more humble as they grow older. They keep finding out how much of a sinner they are and how patient God is with them.

Paul puts it this way. "Here is a trustworthy saying that deserves full acceptance: Christ Jesus came into the world to save sinners—of whom I am the worst. But for that very reason I was shown mercy so that in me, the worst of sinners, Christ Jesus might display his unlimited patience as an example for those who would believe on him and receive eternal life" (1 Timothy 1:15–16).

Here Paul makes a truly daring claim. One would think great leaders like Paul would be able to claim themselves as examples of righteousness and holiness, but Paul does not. He claims quite the opposite;

he brags about being the worst sinner among sinners. He chose to exemplify himself in this manner so that others might have hope. If Christ would have patience with Paul—the worst of sinners—then no sinner could claim to be outside the reach of God's grace.

These are truly unusual bragging rights. In essence Paul is saying *he* has more sin than anyone, so *no one* can have any legitimate reason not to believe in the forgiveness of God. If there's hope for him, the worst of sinners, there's hope for anyone. "For I am the least of the apostles and do not even deserve to be called an apostle, because I persecuted the church of God. But by the grace of God I am what I am, and his grace to me was not without effect" (1 Corinthians 15:9–10).

To extrapolate somewhat on Paul's statement, I offer the following paragraph:

> *You think your sin is so great that God could never forgive you? Well, think again. I murdered Christians for their faith. I carried out the judgment of God upon the very people he was calling out to do his work. The cloaks of the murderers ended up at my feet. Awful things were done, at my command, to more people than I can count who were and are now my brethren, and the responsibility for all these things rests on me.*

More of God, more awareness of sin. The more I see of God, the more I am aware of that in me that is not of God. That's why Paul's statement here is in the present tense: "Christ Jesus came into the world to save sinners—of whom I *am* the worst." Paul experiences a continual awareness of his sin nature. I would want to say I *was* the worst of sinners . . . but not Paul. The reality of his sin was as current and fresh as the reality of God's grace. Paul knew that he couldn't really know God's grace without knowing his sin and how little he deserved what he was receiving. Deserve it, and it is no longer grace.

If we are to recover from this pharisaical phoniness, we are going to have to get a present-tense awareness of our sin. We need to be experts at finding and rooting out our own sin—no one else's. We have plenty to deal with right here in our own heart without having to take on anyone else's sin as our personal campaign. I am the worst sinner I know, simply because I know myself better than anyone. My sin is the worst because it is mine. I am intimately involved with it. I know all its subtle nuances, its illusions, its rationalizations, and its cover-ups. Of my sin I am an expert. Anyone else's sin is not my business to evaluate.

And follow this: Jeremiah informs us that our "expert" knowledge of sin is still limited at best. Deeper than what we know about our sin lies that which we don't know. "The heart is deceitful above all things and beyond cure," cried Jeremiah. "Who can understand it?" (17:9). This is a reminder that, however much we know about our sin, we still do not know it all.

Paul picks up this theme in 1 Corinthians 4:4: "My conscience is clear, but that does not make me innocent. It is the Lord who judges me." Paul never claims sinlessness, but he does claim a clear conscience. The sin Paul knows about, he has brought to the Lord already and received forgiveness; what he doesn't know about is known by God and will be revealed in due time.

A clear conscience, therefore, does not mean we are sinless. It means we are covered by the blood of Jesus for what we know *and* what we don't know. That should keep us humble until the time when the Lord returns. "He will bring to light what is hidden in darkness and expose the motives of men's hearts. At that time each will receive his praise from God" (1 Corinthians 4:5).

## The recovering Pharisee's creed

When I speak of sin, I will no longer talk of it as something in my distant past. When I speak of forgiveness, I will not speak of it as something I received years ago when I became a Christian. I will speak of the sin and forgiveness I experienced today—that I am experiencing right now—that enable me to be human and real and truthful with who I am and who I am becoming. And when conversation turns to talk of sinners, I will realize that the conversation is really about me. I will always know that I am the worst of sinners. *I* put Jesus on the cross; *my* sin nailed him there. And if I ever catch myself thinking that there exists, somewhere in the world, a worse sinner than I, regardless of the gravity of the crime, it is at that point that I have stepped over the pharisaical line and am speaking about something of which I know nothing. When it comes to sin, I can only speak of myself with absolute certainty, and in regard to myself and sin, I am certain of this: that I am an expert in both my sin and my forgiveness. One brings me sorrow; the other brings me great joy. The remarkable thing is not that I sin, but that, in spite of my sin, I am capable of having fellowship with God and being used by him for his purposes in the world.

"So, if you think you are standing firm, be careful that you don't fall!" (1 Corinthians 10:12).

## Pharisees Anonymous

Recovery from any addiction, be it alcohol, drugs, sex, or any other, is never complete. It's never over. That's why there are recovery groups. Recovery groups are there not just to get a person off his dependence on something but to keep him off. Experienced addicts know they are never really "cured," meaning they are never fully outside the risk of succumbing again to their addiction. Alcoholics don't stop being alcoholics; they merely stop drinking, and it's a daily decision.

Sin is very much the same way. We don't cease our struggle with sin when we become saved, as if we were no longer sinners, but we attempt by the power of the Spirit of God in us to stop sinning, and it's a daily decision. Even the attempted cover-up is the same. An alcoholic who is not facing up to his drinking, but is trying to feign a normal life in society as if nothing were wrong, is taking a drink somehow on the sly. In the same way, a Christian who purports to be victorious over sin is hiding something. Pharisees have always been good at disguise.

The recovery model is right at home with the saved sinner. Though it is painful to walk into that room and own up to who we really are, it is comforting and freeing to face the truth and not run away from ourselves anymore. "Hi, I'm John, and I'm a sinner" suddenly becomes not a curse, but an introduction to a group of people who know and are facing with me what that means. This is the sanctification process brought into community. After years of trying and failing to fight sin on our own, we discover we can find help, encouragement, and accountability in others. And these people don't turn you out. They never do. There is no one worse off than anyone else in this group. Tell your story here and it will not shock anyone.

Try it and see how it feels. "Hi, I'm _____, and I'm a sinner." In a true recovery group that announcement would be followed by a hearty "Hi, _____!" from the rest of the group. By this they're saying it's okay, that they understand how it is. Not that sin is okay any more than drunkenness is okay, but rather it's okay in that we're in this battle together and there is hope. There is forgiveness. Others are saying they are sinners too; they want to do something about it just like we do, and that's why we're all here. Doesn't it feel good to be among friends? Doesn't it feel good no longer to have to lie? Don't you wish church could be more like this?

Like church, in any one of these recovery groups, people are at many different levels and stages in their growth. Some have been there for years and are now sponsoring others, helping them get through another day, being available on the phone or at the office when someone is about to go down for the count and needs an immediate hand. Others have just gotten up the nerve to finally walk in the door and have no clue what to expect. They are all in for some love and some understanding, and most of all—some help.

This is also where the church actually has more to offer than a traditional A.A. or other kind of recovery group. Alcoholics Anonymous, where this recovery trend started, in order to maintain a religious ambivalence, can only point addicts to a "Higher Power." The church offers everyone a personal relationship with Jesus Christ, the very one who died to deliver us from our sin. That's pretty hard to beat.

So I'm facing my sin now and getting forgiven and encouraged by other forgiven sinners. I just wish there were something I could do about this propensity toward self-righteousness, now that I've been a Christian for a while. Maybe there is . . .

"Hi, I'm John, and I'm a Pharisee."

**Step 1** We admit that our single most unmitigated pleasure is to judge other people.

**Step 2** Have come to believe that our means of obtaining greatness is to make everyone lower than ourselves in our own mind.

**Step 3** Realize that we detest mercy being given to those who, unlike us, haven't worked for it and don't deserve it.

**Step 4** Have decided that we don't want to get what we deserve after all, and we don't want anyone else to either.

**Step 5** Will cease all attempts to apply teaching and rebuke to anyone but ourselves.

**Step 6** Are ready to have God remove all these defects of attitude and character.

**Step 7** Embrace the belief that we are, and will always be, experts at sinning.

**Step 8** Are looking closely at the lives of famous men and women of the Bible who turned out to be ordinary sinners like us.

**Step 9** Are seeking through prayer and meditation to make a conscious effort to consider others better than ourselves.

**Step 10** Embrace the state of astonishment as a permanent and glorious reality.

**Step 11** Choose to rid ourselves of any attitude that is not bathed in gratitude.

**Step 12** Having had a spiritual awakening as the result of these steps, we will try to carry this message to others who think that Christians are better than everyone else.

STEP 8

*We are looking closely at the lives of famous men and women of the Bible who turned out to be ordinary sinners like us.*

> ( That the scriptures are brim full of
> hustlers, murderers, cowards, adulterers
> and mercenaries used to shock me. Now it
> is a source of great comfort. )
>
> U 2 ' s  B o n o

---

I GREW UP ON BIBLE STORIES. OUR SUNDAY SCHOOL CLASSROOM walls were decorated with biblical artifacts—a construction paper tribute to the valiant exploits of the men and women of faith in the pages of the Old Testament. There were cardboard renditions of David's slingshot that slew Goliath, Samson's jawbone that mowed down a thousand Philistines, Jonah's whale that saved him from a watery grave, Moses' rod that parted the Red Sea, Gideon's trumpet that struck fear into a host of Midianites, Joseph's coat of many colors that camouflaged his flight into Egypt, and, of course, Jacob's ladder that we sang about every week, a ladder that would one day lead us up into heaven as soldiers of the cross.

We celebrated these heroes and their stories each week in church, midweek in someone's home for child evangelism, and in the summer there was vacation Bible school, where each year a Bible story became the theme for a two-week biblical adventure. We dressed like Bible characters, colored in their pictures, moved their figures around on a flannelgraph board, and made paper-mache replicas of their boats, their weapons, their cities, and the walls of their enemy's fortresses that fell down flat every time we marched around them (seven times, of course).

These were our heroes, not the sports figures, rock stars, and television and movie celebrities that would later adorn our walls. These heroes hung on the walls of our minds and captured our childhood imagination—each of them representing something great for us to admire and emulate. Solomon was the wisest, Samson was the strongest, Jacob was the cleverest, Gideon was the bravest, Jonah was the luckiest, Moses was the boldest, Joshua was the most courageous, and David was the greatest of them all, because he defeated the giant Goliath with nothing but a slingshot as a little boy no older than we were then.

But alas, these pictures, like childhood itself, could not remain so naïve. As I grew up, it seemed these characters grew along with me into the same ambiguities and inconsistencies I was forced to face as I adjusted to an adult world. At some point I found out the rest of the story, and the rest of the story was not so good.

At some point in my life I had to face the disappointing fact that Solomon was a bigamist, Samson was a womanizer, Jacob was a deceiver, Gideon was an idolater, David was an adulterer and murderer, and Jonah was running away from God even after he got to Nineveh. When I finally was old enough to read these stories for myself and see beyond the grid of my preconceived Sunday school notions, my heroic, grand illusions gradually began to resemble more of a Bible soap opera than anything else, complete with juicy details of lust, jealousy, backstabbing, and betrayal. These people didn't float down to earth lightly, they fell with a great crash, and the sound of it echoed down the corridors of my Bible hall of fame.

Did this other side of the story crush my idealism? Did finding out about these human weaknesses and sinful lapses endanger my faith? Actually I was surprised to find that these discoveries were, more than anything, a very great relief. Instead of losing heart, I gained it. The more messed-up these Bible heroes turned out to be, the better I felt. Not that I had somehow turned sadistic in my assessments; I was simply relieved to find out how human and fallible these people were, after all. Some of them were guilty of things I have never even thought about doing. And yet in spite of this God worked with them. He loved them, spoke highly of them, and put them to use for his kingdom. They were still heroes to me, only in a different way. No longer heroes for their outstanding human attributes; they were heroes for their faith—

faith in spite of their foibles and fallibilities. I saw them in a different light because I was learning that God operates through human imperfection. He does not model perfect Herculean examples; he models faithful human ones. I ended up liking these biblical characters more than before. Once they were heroes of faith to aspire to but never reach; now they were heroes of faith who were not that much different than me.

I have to admit I have a certain distaste for Sunday school and the false teachers who disseminated these lies. I would rather they had brought these people down to earth for us even as children so we wouldn't have had to relearn so much later. I know it's harsh to call them false teachers—they were most likely volunteers who followed a course curriculum—but just the same, someone must have known they were telling us half-truths, and half-truths can be worse than lies if they end up teaching you something that God never intended to teach. These characters were never meant to be showcased for their wisdom, cleverness, bravery, and strength. They were to be examples of what God can do through whomever he chooses.

## Read your Bible . . . and go figure

The first thing one notices about the story of Samson, for instance, is that most of his victories over the Philistines sprang from illicit relationships with Philistine women strictly forbidden by Jewish law. "Must you go to the uncircumcised Philistines to get a wife?" his parents objected. But then the Scripture goes on to say, "His parents did not know that this was from the Lord, who was seeking an occasion to confront the Philistines" (Judges 14:3–4). Later, after killing a lion, Samson ate honey from its dead carcass—a miracle produced by God that lead him to ignore another Jewish law about touching something dead. In other words, Samson was breaking the rules right and left, and what's more, he appeared to be encouraged to do so by God. Many times in this account, when Samson got himself into compromising situations, the Bible says, "The Spirit of the Lord came upon him. . . ." Strange company for the Spirit of the Lord.

Mixed in with Samson's great exploits against the Philistines were his apparent free-ranging relationships with prostitutes. After avenging the death of his first wife, God used Samson's weakness for Philistine women to keep trapping him in situations where he had to take out a few hundred Philistine warriors in order to extricate himself. Though he conquered many enemies with his strength, his finest motivations never rose above lust, jealousy, and revenge. These were the things God used in Samson's life to judge the Philistines during a time when they were ruling over Israel.

Couldn't God have instilled something a bit higher in Samson as a motivation—something with some character that would have been a little more appropriate for Sunday school so our teachers could have told us the whole story? He probably could have but he didn't. Why he didn't is cause for speculation, but it still remains that God delivered his people through a sinful man who behaved with little or no regard for the right thing to do. And the Spirit of God associated with this kind of irresponsible behavior. Read the Bible and go figure.

Does this mean that God condones these things? Of course not. Does it mean that God can accomplish his purposes in spite of these things? Of course it does.

## Liar, liar . . .

Jacob is another interesting study in God's questionable alliances with fallible people. Jacob's name literally means "he grasps the heel," which refers to his holding onto his brother's foot as he emerged from the womb minutes behind him. Jacob figuratively means "he deceives," which appropriately describes his character. He was a schemer—a "smooth man," says the King James Version, as opposed to his brother Esau, who was a "hairy man." "Smooth" as in "slick." That was Jacob. He was a conniver and a trickster—a smooth operator at best. He tricked his brother out of his birthright and his blessing (Genesis 27) even though he was the second-born, and then, as a true coward, he ran away as soon as his brother found out. And God blessed Jacob and made him the father of the Jewish nation. His name later was changed to Israel. Anyone ever wonder how this works . . . how God manages to bless this?

And what of his mother, Rebekah? She was a major accomplice in his deception. She was the one who in the first place concocted the idea of having Jacob serve up her blind husband's favorite stew in Esau's clothes so Isaac would smell the smell of Esau and bless Jacob instead. All the while Jacob was lying through his teeth.

"Who is it?" Isaac asks.

"I am Esau, your firstborn," says Jacob. "Please sit up and eat some of my game so that you may give me my blessing."

"How did you find it so quickly?" (He had just sent Esau out to find game and cook a stew.)

"The Lord your God gave me success," said Jacob, and it's a wonder God didn't strike him down right there on the spot. But he didn't. And not only that, God blessed Jacob and honored Isaac's blessing obtained by violating at least two of the Ten Commandments—not to steal or bear false witness. (What Jacob did was not too honoring to his father, either, which could account for a third violation.) In other words, God's will took into account the sinfulness of Jacob and his mother. You could go as far as to say it depended on it. God could have just as easily made Jacob the firstborn and none of this would have had to happen, but he designed it this way. He made Jacob the second-born and then worked through the lying, stealing, and manipulating of Jacob and Rebekah to reorder the arrangement. You can do theological and cultural gymnastics until you are tied up in knots, but you are never going to straighten this one out. This is, pure and simple, God working though people with serious faults—people like you and me.

Does this mean that God condones these things? Of course not. Does it mean that God can accomplish his purposes in spite of these things? Of course it does.

Sometimes I wonder if it might be that liars and manipulators and thieves and avengers are the only kinds of people he has to work with. Or maybe these are the people he *wants* to work with. Could it be that God chose people like this because he'd rather work with those who know their glaring faults than with Pharisees who are impressed with their own righteousness and God's excellent choice in choosing them?

## The last laugh

Abraham's wife, Sarah, is perhaps a more accessible representative for many of us. Her sins and weaknesses are a bit more subtle. We can even envision ourselves doing the same things, given the same circumstances. I don't know about you, but it's not my style to hang out with prostitutes and avenge myself on their jealous lovers, but I could see myself lying just a little bit to save my skin or to get something I really wanted. Not a big lie like Jacob's, but a little one like Sarah's.

It was Abraham's idea, but she went along with it. "As he was about to enter Egypt, he said to his wife [then known as Sarai], 'I know what a beautiful woman you are. When the Egyptians see you, they will say, "This is his wife." Then they will kill me but will let you live. Say you are my sister, so that I will be treated well for your sake and my life will be spared because of you'" (Genesis 12:11–13).

Which is exactly what she did. As Abraham predicted, Pharaoh noticed her beauty and brought her into his palace and gave Abraham, her supposed brother, gifts of livestock and servants until a plague came upon Pharaoh and his household and he figured out it was because he had unwittingly taken in another man's wife.

"Why didn't you tell me she was your wife?" Pharaoh demanded of Abraham. "Why did you say, 'She is my sister,' so that I took her to be my wife? Now then, here is your wife. Take her and go!" (Genesis 12:18–19) Even pagan kings have scruples.

The next episode in the life of Sarah happened years later, as it was becoming harder and harder for her to believe God's promise to Abraham to make him the father of many nations when he wasn't even the father of a son (Genesis 16–18). So Sarah, barren and desperate, gave Abraham her maidservant, Hagar, that he might have the promised child through her. The plan backfired. No sooner was Hagar pregnant than Sarah became overcome with jealousy and the two women despised each other. Sarah ended up mistreating Hagar so much that she had to flee.

This time the manipulation that worked for Rebekah didn't work for Sarah. There are no patterns in these things. Some try to dance through these Old Testament stories and make them fit neatly into the laws and principles they want us to build our lives on, but the stories refuse to fit. That's because our lives are not built on laws and principles; they are built on a consistent, compassionate God who somehow works in and around our human failures to work his perfect will in our imperfect lives.

So it was that when Sarah overheard three visitors telling Abraham many years later that the next year when they returned, they would find Abraham holding a newborn son by his wife, she laughed. It was not a joyous laugh. It was not the laughter of faith. It was the laughter of sarcasm—a cynical laugh, brewing over years of bitterness and uncontrollably spilling out of her mouth upon hearing such preposterous news. "After I am worn out and my master is old, will I now have this pleasure?" she said to herself. She had tried to conceal the laugh, but one of the visitors heard.

"Why did Sarah laugh?" he said to Abraham. "Is anything too hard for the Lord?"

Sarah was afraid, so she lied and said, "I did not laugh."

But he said, "Yes, you did laugh."

And we know who had the last laugh.

## Cowardly overconfident

Sometimes even as adults we have a hard time facing the whole truth about these Bible characters. Our pharisaical thinking is so ingrained in us that we can't read such stories without blinders on. We excuse their indiscretions on cultural differences or translations from the original languages. We continue to believe that God uses "good" people. We simply have a hard time finding drunks, cheats, liars, womanizers, adulterers, and murderers on God's Favorite People list.

Shouldn't these be stories about good people doing great things for God? Then we could hold motivational seminars and inspire everybody to greatness. That's the way we would do it. "But God chose the foolish things of the world to shame the wise; God chose the weak things of the world to shame the strong. He chose the lowly things of this world and the despised things—and the things that are not—to nullify the things that are, so that no one may boast before him" (1 Corinthians 1:27–29).

God chose Gideon when he was hiding from the invading Midianites in a winepress. Gideon immediately balked at God's choice. "How can I save Israel? My clan is the weakest in Manasseh, and I am the least in my family." Not exactly heroic material. Three miraculous signs and one prophetic dream later, Gideon finally got the courage to go up against the Midianites. That was after first purging his own camp of its idols, "but because he was afraid of his family and the men of the town, he did it at night rather than in the daytime" (Judges 6:27).

As a coward, bolstered by God's miraculous visitations, Gideon goes forth against the enemy, reduced by God's instructions to a small band of men, so small that no victory could be had without God's direct intervention. When that intervention took place, and Gideon, buoyed by his new successes, turned into a vindictive warrior, plundering, punishing, and personally killing neighboring kings, suddenly he appears dangerously close to going perhaps a little too far in the other direction.

As it turned out, what began well had a sour finish. Gideon's account in Scripture concludes with his saying the right thing and then going right ahead and doing the wrong thing. When the Israelites, fresh from victory, wanted to make him their ruler, Gideon replied, "I will not rule over you, nor will my son rule over you. The Lord will rule over you."

Way to go, Gideon. Well said! Bravo, you've learned your lesson. But no sooner was this out of his mouth than he followed it up with, "I do have one request, that each of you give me an earring from your share of the plunder." (It was the custom of the people they had just conquered to wear gold earrings.) And what did he do with all those earrings? He melted them down and made an ephod (a sculpted replica of a high-priestly garment) that he placed in the center of his town, and "all Israel prostituted themselves by worshiping it there, and it became a snare to Gideon and his family."

I'll bet no one learned that part of the story in Sunday school. No one talked about how the story ended. No one made a point of Gideon's snare, only Gideon's victory against all odds. Yet it's there in black and white, in your Bible and mine, a story of success depending on the Lord followed by failure depending on self and pride, and cushioned by newly gained wealth. This story is more than a study in discovering God's strength; it is a study in carrying God's victory too far. Like all these stories, it is a story of human greatness and human failure all wrapped up together.

## The whole story

If the Bible tells the whole story, then we need to tell the whole story, too, about our own lives. We tell the whole story about our successes and our failures for the same reason these stories are in Scripture. We tell the whole story so that it becomes very clear to anyone who might care to notice that we are not the heroes of the message we bring and the stories we tell. We are participants in the Story of which Jesus Christ is the beginning, the middle, and the end.

We get it right sometimes and we get it wrong sometimes. When we get it right, it is because we are depending on God's strength and presence in our lives, not on anything in and of ourselves. When we get it wrong, it is because we are looking to ourselves and either cowering in a winepress for fear of defeat or overconfident in the victory itself and not in God.

Need I go on about the nakedness of Noah, the futility of Solomon, the impatience of Moses, the compromise of Saul, the wickedness of Eli's sons, the self-righteousness of Job, the sorrow of David, the brazenness of Abigail, the quirkiness of John the Baptist, the denial of Peter, the defection of John Mark, the argument between Peter and Paul, the sickness of Timothy, the doubting of Thomas, or the thorn in the flesh of the great apostle? All these stories make faith real and possible for every one of us because we see ourselves, or parts of ourselves, between their pages. They are stories of doubt and faith, of struggle and release, of pain and pleasure, of victory and defeat. Most of all they are stories that read like our lives and give us courage, not because they are about great people whom we admire, but because they are about ordinary people who have a great God.

**Step 1** We admit that our single most unmitigated pleasure is to judge other people.

**Step 2** Have come to believe that our means of obtaining greatness is to make everyone lower than ourselves in our own mind.

**Step 3** Realize that we detest mercy being given to those who, unlike us, haven't worked for it and don't deserve it.

**Step 4** Have decided that we don't want to get what we deserve after all, and we don't want anyone else to either.

**Step 5** Will cease all attempts to apply teaching and rebuke to anyone but ourselves.

**Step 6** Are ready to have God remove all these defects of attitude and character.

**Step 7** Embrace the belief that we are, and will always be, experts at sinning.

**Step 8** Are looking closely at the lives of famous men and women of the Bible who turned out to be ordinary sinners like us.

**Step 9** Are seeking through prayer and meditation to make a conscious effort to consider others better than ourselves.

**Step 10** Embrace the state of astonishment as a permanent and glorious reality.

**Step 11** Choose to rid ourselves of any attitude that is not bathed in gratitude.

**Step 12** Having had a spiritual awakening as the result of these steps, we will try to carry this message to others who think that Christians are better than everyone else.

S T E P

We are seeking
through prayer and
meditation to make
a conscious effort
to consider others
better than ourselves.

> I became a servant of this gospel by the gift of God's grace given me through the working of his power. Although I am less than the least of all God's people, this grace was given me.
>
> THE APOSTLE PAUL

---

YOUR IGNORANCE IS EXCEEDED ONLY BY YOUR [EXPLETIVE deleted]."

This comment was directed at me and came from a total stranger. He had been listening in on a conversation I was having in a New York diner with five students from a nearby Christian college where I was a guest speaker. After noticing his ear turned in our direction and watching him grow more and more agitated, I turned to him and invited his comment. The emotional outburst that ensued caught our table totally by surprise. He surmised I was a professor and chided me for acting like an expert on things I knew nothing about. And then he concluded with the above comment that put my knowledge on a par with what male bovine leave behind in a pasture.

Needless to say, his tirade froze and embarrassed our table. His comment and unfounded anger seemed to come from out of nowhere. After a few moments of uncomfortable silence, a young female student, who was closest to him, pulled her chair over to try to talk with the man. She was very meek and sensitive—an unlikely one to be the first to respond to him—but she had noticed earlier that a book he had with him was, of all things, a modern paraphrase of the Bible.

As it turned out, the man was a Christian, albeit a highly

opinionated one, and he had completely misconstrued our conversation after overhearing only a few words. Our table emissary proceeded to correct his misunderstanding, and as we stood up to leave shortly thereafter, he shook hands all around and apologized profusely. He was quite chagrined to find out we were all Christians and appeared to regret both his outburst and his choice of words.

As we drove away from the diner, there was a tendency in our group to discount the man's assessment of me by way of his rush to judgment and his unchristian-like attitude. The students were embarrassed for me, and the most readily available path toward recovering some dignity was to disregard the man by the way he represented himself. What sort of Christian would display such an attitude in front of total strangers?

I, on the other hand, was troubled by something else. The more I thought about what the man had said, the more I began to be convicted by it. He may have gotten the content of our conversation wrong, but he had spotted something true about the way I was interacting with the group of students at my table. Putting myself in his place, I could see how he might have come to his conclusions about me.

Many of my personal appearances at Christian colleges around the country have a similar format. Two or three chapel presentations are followed up by more informal small group discussions in classrooms, dorm lounges, and the dining hall, or, as was the case here, in a restaurant off campus. In these sessions, students react to the issues I raise in chapel—often somewhat thorny issues that I know will get them thinking and stimulate discussion. These discussions usually fall into a question-and-answer format with questions coming from students, and answers—of course—coming from me. I began to realize as we were driving back to campus that the man was most likely reacting to my arrogance at having an answer for everything. Well, he was right. I do get used to this type of interaction, and my position can become a source of pride. He may have wrongly assessed the content of our conversation, but he had correctly interpreted its attitude.

From the moment I get off a plane to appear somewhere as a guest speaker/singer to the moment I reboard, I am "somebody" by way of a picture, a bio, and an honorarium fee. People who have been anticipating my coming and have arranged to meet my needs during the time I am with them surround me. Funny, I never get treated like this at home. At home nobody gives a second thought to my being any more special than anyone else in the family. At home I have to care about those around me in order to get by; on the road, people seem to care about me without needing me to care in return. They ask me questions; they want to know what I think; and I am eager to oblige. In fact, I thrive on this attention. This can easily become addictive, to where I am looking forward to the next time I leave so I can feel important again.

Most of us have something we excel in—some talent or expertise we possess—that sets us apart from everyone else, even if only for a moment, a day, or a weekend. If we make these the defining moments in our lives, we may get a false sense of our importance. And if we use this expertise as proof of our worth, we are only getting part of the story.

I believe I was operating from a false sense of worth that evening in the diner, and the man at the next table saw it and called my bluff. I was acting like my opinion was the only one that mattered. I was the one worth hearing. I was the one to whom all questions were being addressed. I was in my element. But there were five other people with me at that table; what about them? Who probed their thoughts and opinions? Who explored their arguments? What did I walk away knowing about the people at that table that I didn't know when I sat down? Unfortunately, very little. My thoughts and my opinions were the theme of that conversation. I did not enrich myself with the thoughts and opinions of those around me; I merely rehashed my own well-worn ones. I deserved the man's assessment . . . perhaps even his language.

## Looking out for #2

Paul says, "Do nothing out of selfish ambition or vain conceit, but in humility consider others better than yourselves. Each of you should look not only to your own interests, but also to the interests of others" (Philippians 2:3–4). This is the opposite of Step 2. Instead of putting people down, we put them up, and we do this by taking a secondary, supportive role to those around us.

This is not a false, groveling humility; it is a way of considering others that elevates them. It's all about learning to appreciate those around us, giving validity to their opinions and points of view. It's all about giving someone else your seat, taking the last place in line instead of shoving through to the front, listening instead of waiting to talk, going the extra mile, bending over backwards, and not looking out for number one but, instead, looking out for number two.

There's one sure way to consider other people as better than yourself and that is to truly believe that they are. You can't fake this. You can't act as if it were true while all along you suspect that it is not. How do you do this? How do you make some scoundrel better than you? You go back to Step 7 and review your own sinful condition and then remember: you are an expert at spotting your own sin but not very good at seeing anyone else's. Their sin is not your business. You can't see someone else's heart anyway. You don't know what's really going on. You only know what's going on with you—where God is rooting out your latest compromise or your most clever rationalization. You're too busy with your own sin to worry about anyone else's and so, because you see yourself as the "least of the least," the other guy is always better than you.

This is elementary, but a way to avoid putting people down is to put them up instead. Ask the question: "What do they have that I need? What are they good at?" I believe now that the man in the diner had insight about me that I needed. He had a perspective I didn't have and could see me better than I could see myself at the time.

## What they could be/What you would be

Another way to do this is to see other people not as what they are but as what they could be in Christ. This gives us a means of appreciating someone even when it is hard to find something to appreciate.

Paul says that love believes all things, and that sometimes means believing the impossible for someone else. By doing this, we can often create an environment for people to change.

My mother is slowly losing her mind. Call it dementia, call it Alzheimer's; I call it being eighty-nine. Where she used to be engaging, with a mind as sharp as a tack, she now retreats into silence when around others, even members of her family, most of whom she no longer recognizes. She has lost all confidence in her ability to speak. Her sentences begin promisingly but trail off quickly into a repetitive dead end, like words rattling around in a cage.

I have taken to calling her on occasion and talking with her on the phone. For this I have developed a means of communicating. First, I never correct her; I go wherever she wants to go. When she veers off track into gibberish, I say something that brings her back to where she got off, and in this manner some semblance of a conversation is pieced together. While doing this, I write down every word she says as fast as I can, even the ones that don't make sense. It has always happened that later, when I go over the three or four pages of notes I have taken, a message emerges. It is never the same, and always it is something I needed to hear, personally.

My father says she brightens when I call. Maybe that's because I don't berate her for not making sense, nor do I try to straighten out her sentences. I treat her as if she were making sense. I'm not bragging about this—I probably would not have this patience if I had to bear the frustration of living with her every day—I'm merely noticing that believing all things about someone and treating them accordingly is a very powerful force.

When we see others as they could be in Christ, we are creating an environment for it to be so. Not that we make it so by believing it, but our faith may help open a way. Like palm branches before the triumphant Christ, we can pave the road for some new form of "Hosanna" should Christ choose to come this way.

It is a good axiom, well worth considering, to see others as what they could be in Christ, while seeing yourself as what you would be without him. On this basis, we will always see others as better than ourselves.

## Everyone's a star

My wife is incredible at this. She has a spiritual gift: an ability to make everyone around her shine. She finds out what makes each person unique and affirms them for that. She can work a room like nobody's business (sometimes it is her business), and when she leaves it, eyes are brighter, steps are lighter—and this is genuine. It's as if she has made her way around the room and handed each person a gift—a gift they already possessed. She has found something about them, buffed it to a shine, held it up to the light, and handed it back to them. Years ago, when she used to fly for United Airlines, ticket agents could immediately identify one of Marti's flights by the smiles on the people coming off a plane. I understand why. I have seen this magic at work time and time again and have been the recipient of it myself. She does this without trying. Though this behavior used to baffle me, I realize now that it's not very complicated. I will admit she has a special gift for this, but it's also something the rest of us can learn. It's as simple as what Paul told us to do: to consider everyone else as more important than ourselves or, as Marti would do, to make everyone else a star. I may have been the star of the night at that diner in New York, but I could have seen that a galaxy surrounded me.

This is not easy to do. It runs against the grain of our natural inclinations. We are much more talented and experienced at finding faults in people than we are at finding admirable qualities. The man in the diner, in spite of his attitude, had admirable qualities, but it was his abrasiveness that was the easiest to attach to him. If I could see him again, I would thank him. I might even desire him as a friend, if I had the nerve. He would be the type of friend who would not let me get away with anything. He would tell me the truth about myself, and I'm sure it would hurt just as much as it hurt that night to have my lights punched out.

## Searchin' for a heart of gold...

"Whatever is true, whatever is noble, whatever is right, whatever is pure, whatever is lovely, whatever is admirable—if anything is excellent or praiseworthy—think about such things" (Philippians 4:8). I used to think these qualities were intrinsic in some things and not in others, so that this call of the apostle became a way of arranging the good and the bad things in life. I worry, however, that such an interpretation further compartmentalizes an already fragmented existence. I since have come to believe that Paul was not asking us to arrange our world so as to be always surrounded by holy things, but to find what is worthwhile in everything we do and everyone we meet. This is not a way of assessing right and wrong things in the world as much as it is a way of extracting from everything that which is useful to our faith. I believe it was meant to be applied to people as well.

That means I can look and listen for what is noble and admirable in everyone around me. Everyone. Even the unseemly, such as non-Christians, nerds, political enemies, murderers, fascists, and the profane. We look across at eye level to everyone. Something can be found even in the fallen. There is no place we can relegate the scumbags of the world. Only God can do that. Our responsibility is to look for what is redeemable.

During the writing of this book, two teenage boys took to killing themselves in a Littleton, Colorado, high school and taking twelve of their classmates and a teacher along with them to a violent death. Their diaries indicated that they failed greatly. Their goal had been five hundred deaths. The tendency since this tragedy has been to demonize these two, which is easily understandable, their deed being so incomprehensible and so full of design and premeditation as to be the epitome of evil and beyond belief. The news media continually referred to the two as "shooters," "gunmen," and "killers," yet they were but children, still teenagers themselves—each one still some mother's little boy.

As the shock and horror surrounding this event settled in on a nation, there appeared to be two different reactions to the two boys who were responsible for such mayhem. One was to cast blame somewhere—on them, their parents, the violence of the media, the school for not noticing, their peers for not telling. Another, less popular reaction, was to take on the blame. This reaction was stated most eloquently in a note that was tacked to the cross of the boy who seemed the ringleader and the one most responsible for engineering the deadly scheme. It read, "You were lost long before you died. Forgive us for not noticing." Only those able to consider others as better than themselves would see this option. Pharisees cast blame; recovering Pharisees take blame. Jesus would have taken it. That's what his cross was all about.

## Looking up to tax collectors

To some who were confident of their own righteousness and looked down on everybody else, Jesus told this parable: "Two men went up to the temple to pray, one a Pharisee and the other a tax collector. The Pharisee stood up and prayed about himself: 'God, I thank you that I am not like other men—robbers, evildoers, adulterers—or even like this tax collector. I fast twice a week and give a tenth of all I get.'

"But the tax collector stood at a distance. He would not even look up to heaven, but beat his breast and said, 'God, have mercy on me, a sinner.'

"I tell you that this man, rather than the other, went home justified before God. For everyone who exalts himself will be humbled, and he who humbles himself will be exalted" (Luke 18:9–14).

The striking thing about this story is the relationship of the tax collector and God, and the tragedy that keeps the Pharisee from knowing it for himself. What the Pharisee doesn't recognize is that the tax collector, whom he despises, has God's attention. But because he must put the tax collector down in order to maintain his idea of righteousness, he, in his pride and arrogance, will never know what the tax collector knows. If he counted the tax collector as better than himself, if he even held out the slightest possibility that someone in such a lowly position just might have something to teach him, there could have been hope for the Pharisee. But as long as a Pharisee stays confident in his own righteousness, he will never see God.

What the tax collector has to offer the Pharisee is what the poor always have to offer the rich: a clear sight of what is truly important in life. In this way the poor and the sinners are "better" than the rich and the righteous. And Jesus was always on their side. If a Pharisee wants to recover, a good place to begin would be to look up to those he or she formerly would have judged.

I have had the privilege on a few occasions to sing to Christian inmates in prison and be taught by them. To be in the presence of men and women behind bars who know God and experience true freedom is a humbling experience. I've never done this when I didn't wonder on what side of the bars I was really on. It's a strange feeling to be dwarfed by the spirituality of prisoners and bound by the cares and pleasures of the world that taunt me incessantly. They have so little of what the world offers but so much of God. I, in turn, have so much of what the world offers, and often experience so little of God. I have much to learn from these people.

Paul considered himself "less than the least of all God's people." From that vantage point, he would be looking up to everyone—even tax collectors.

*Step 1* We admit that our single most unmitigated pleasure is to judge other people.

*Step 2* Have come to believe that our means of obtaining greatness is to make everyone lower than ourselves in our own mind.

*Step 3* Realize that we detest mercy being given to those who, unlike us, haven't worked for it and don't deserve it.

*Step 4* Have decided that we don't want to get what we deserve after all, and we don't want anyone else to either.

*Step 5* Will cease all attempts to apply teaching and rebuke to any-one but ourselves.

*Step 6* Are ready to have God remove all these defects of attitude and character.

*Step 7* Embrace the belief that we are, and will always be, experts at sinning.

*Step 8* Are looking closely at the lives of famous men and women of the Bible who turned out to be ordinary sinners like us.

*Step 9* Are seeking through prayer and meditation to make a con-scious effort to consider others better than ourselves.

*Step 10* Embrace the state of astonishment as a permanent and glorious reality.

*Step 11* Choose to rid ourselves of any attitude that is not bathed in gratitude.

*Step 12* Having had a spiritual awakening as the result of these steps, we will try to carry this message to others who think that Christians are better than everyone else.

We embrace the
state of astonishment
as a permanent and
glorious reality.

What have I ever done to deserve
Even one of the pleasures I've known?
What did I ever do that was worth lovin' you,
For the kindness you've shown?

K R I S   K R I S T O F F E R S O N

---

Søren Kierkegaard, that strange and sometimes hard to understand Danish philosopher of a century ago, somewhere says that the way to become authentically Christian is to take any one of Jesus' precepts and try to keep it. He didn't mean it would be easy to do and all of us would become better believers as a result. He rather meant that if we try to follow any particular teaching, we'll be driven to confession of our own sinfulness and the need for continual forgiveness. "It is a consoling idea," wrote Kierkegaard, "that we are always in the wrong."

The above paragraph by David Roper from an Internet study on the book of James points to a strange and wonderful consolation. Being always in the wrong is a source of consolation because it renders fruitless forever the act of trying to be anything else. For recovering Pharisees, there can be no greater news than the announcement that everything they have been trying to do to better themselves, for however long they have been trying to do it, is completely and utterly ineffectual. What they were trying to achieve is an ethical and moral impossibility. If it were even remotely possible—say, one Pharisee per generation could actually earn righteousness as a reward for good behavior—then there would be reason enough to try. But the whole sys-

130

tem collapses in the elimination of the possibility.

This is why Jesus' reinterpretation of the law in the Sermon on the Mount (as something no one could perfectly perform) was the most gracious thing he could do for Pharisees. He was offering them consolation—a way out. He was doing them a favor, even though as far as the New Testament record indicates, it's possible that the only one who recognized it as such was Nicodemus. The only way to save a Pharisee is to break a Pharisee's back with the burden of law. There was, and is, hope for the Pharisee, and that hope comes in the form of failure. Failure is the doorway to freedom, but of course this presents a huge dilemma, since failure is the one thing a good Pharisee can never accept.

## Some consolation

"All who rely on observing the law are under a curse, for it is written: 'Cursed is everyone who does not continue to do everything written in the Book of the Law'" (Galatians 3:10). And everything means *everything*. There can be no lapse. No forgiveness. No room to bend. Law has no grace. We are talking completely error-free ball here not for a season, but for an entire career. No lustful thought, no angry word, not one lie, and this, *in a whole lifetime*—not just from the time we decided to be righteous. Perhaps if Pharisees knew this going in, they might have second thoughts about joining up. Then again, the adjustments of the law and rationalizations of the mind are powerful addictions. When we are in control of our own spirituality, we are hooked on it.

But the curse of the Pharisees, as Kierkegaard pointed out, is also their cure. If a Pharisee is going to get free, this is where it will begin, in realizing that the true demands of righteousness are beyond reach. The whole system is a sham. Righteousness, as it has been explained and modeled by those within the system, is a bad copy of the original. The original can only be produced by the Original. In other words, righteousness can only come via the Spirit of God, and the Spirit of God can only come to forgiven sinners who have claimed total spiritual bankruptcy.

### *"May I have the envelope, please?"*

"Blessed are the poor in spirit, for theirs is the kingdom of heaven. Blessed are those who mourn, for they will be comforted. Blessed are the meek, for they will inherit the earth. Blessed are those who hunger and thirst for righteousness, for they will be filled" (Matthew 5:3–6).

As a child growing up in an upper middle-class evangelical church, I had a terrible time making sense of these opening words of the Lord's first official sermon in the New Testament. I can remember thinking that it must be about God being nice to poor people. How else do you explain a statement about the poor being blessed in a church that was spiritually and economically affluent? None of the Christians I knew were poor, or mourning anything, or meek people wishing they could be more righteous. They were already all spiritual giants as far as I knew; at least no one told me differently. And if my church was full of people already blessed, then who was Jesus talking about here? Beats me. Perhaps the blessing wasn't for us, or maybe we had already gotten it. Either way, this part of the message never seemed to apply to me.

I do remember a slight pang, however, at wondering why Christ would begin something as important as his first recorded sermon with a statement that didn't apply to everyone. It wasn't until years later that I realized Jesus meant exactly what he said and he meant it for everybody. It is only the spiritually bankrupt, the sorrowful, the humble, and the unrighteous who get the blessing. (You have to be unrighteous, by the way, in order to hunger and thirst for righteousness. Already righteous people don't need *more* righteousness.) Needy people get the blessing because they get the point. *They* are the poor and mournful and meek and hungry. They are the ones Jesus is talking about. And they are not this way only for a while until they get blessed; *they are this way all the time.* They get the point that the blessings of God come only to losers. They are consoled in the knowledge that they are always wrong, for their failure to measure up continually qualifies them for the blessing—not because of their goodness, but because of their desperate need for it.

Losing is the only thing that will let us off the hook. It's not just that we all lose at one time or another; we're *supposed* to lose because we are, all of us, *losers*. That's what the law was for in the first place, to show us up for who we really are. The Pharisees sabotaged the whole plan by turning the law into something attainable. *God* sent the law to show us what wicked sinners we are; the *Pharisees* short-circuited the whole process by receiving the law and saying instead, "Hey, wait a minute. We can do this." Of course, God said, "No, you cannot," but they didn't hear him. They were already off somewhere on their own trying to make the law work for them. They never discovered Kierkegaard's remedy, that they were always in the wrong—the remedy that would have led them to Christ (Galatians 3:24).

I'm sure that when the Pharisees heard the opening to the Sermon on the Mount, they did the same thing I did—they figured Jesus was talking about somebody else. It didn't bother them, of course; they didn't need the blessing anyway. Just like I didn't need it, being that I was from such a spiritually endowed church and family.

Something happened to change my mind. It didn't happen all at once. It took some time, some growing up, some desperation, some depression, and my own healthy share of selfishness and sin to realize it, but this Pharisee finally saw his pharisaical spirituality for the farce that it always is and always was. This is when the glorious truth dawned on me. I qualified! I was the poor, sad sinner Jesus was talking about, and that could mean only one thing: I was blessed. My loss was my gain.

It always happens that just when we think we are really messing up something terrible, we find, instead, our entry into a permanent state of astonishment. Finally we give up and the truth breaks in on us in all its inexplicable glory. This is when the surprise hits, and it is completely paradoxical to the way we have thought and operated all our lives. We give up and we get it. We lose and we win. We greet our poverty and God opens the windows of heaven and greets us with his blessing. We hand ourselves over and get ourselves back. Suddenly we realize that the Sermon on the Mount was all about us.

This is the mystery of the gospel. In a lecture, Robert Farrar Capon states this mystery, in all its paradoxical whimsy:

[The gospel] is not a question to be answered or a puzzle to be solved. It is a paradox to be relished, a wild, outrageous secret to be astonished at and then snitched to the world as the greatest joke ever told. . . . The Mystery of Christ is a festival of weakness and foolishness on the part of God . . . something that makes no more sense than the square root of minus one—something that is deaf to our cries for intelligible explanations but that works when it is put into the equation of the world—something that can only be marveled at because it is such preposterously Good News. The Bible, from Genesis to Revelation, has one Word for us: God has upped and done the damnedest thing. Or, to get the direction and adjectives right, God has downed and done the blessedest thing we could ever *not* have thought of.

Why would we have never thought of the gospel? Because it is backwards to the way we naturally operate. From childhood on, we have always earned our place in life. We have learned that good performances are rewarded and poor performances are punished. How does one suddenly receive something so wonderful that has nothing to do whatsoever with performance? It's not easy. In fact this reverse nature of the gospel is one of the simplest arguments for the validity of Christianity: no human being would have ever thought this up. Who has ever thought of a false gospel with a free gift of salvation? Hasn't happened and it's not going to happen. All false gospels are based on works because that's what we're after. The gift of salvation is simply too preposterous for our imagination.

## Who could have thought?

This is the first blessing: *The relief of facing the truth about ourselves.* The system won't work; it was never designed to work; it was actually designed to bring us ultimately to the realization that it *can't* work. And what the law couldn't do, grace did. "For if a law had been given that could impart life, then righteousness would certainly have come by the law. But the Scripture declares that the whole world is a prisoner of sin, so that what was promised, being given through faith in Jesus Christ, might be given to those who believe" (Galatians 3:21–22).

Which brings us to the second blessing: *The realization that nothing can be done.* Nothing can be added. Nothing can be earned. Nothing can be taken away. Just as law has no grace, grace has no law. "Christ is the end of the law so that there may be righteousness for everyone who believes" (Romans 10:4). Even if you wanted to contribute to your righteousness, you couldn't.

We can't help but be amazed. This is Ebenezer Scrooge after discovering the amazing ghosts have done it all in one night and he still has Christmas Day to make up for all the Christmases he missed. This is gimpy Kirk Gibson in his only at-bat in the 1988 World Series, with cortisone in both knees, pumping his fist in the air as he hobbles around all four bases, making us all wonder how on earth he managed to come off the bench and deliver a game-winning home run with his underdog team down to its last strike. This is Alice in Wonderland, Cinderella at the ball, David dancing before the ark. This is a Pharisee giddy with delight, laughing for perhaps the first time in his life. He's laughing at himself. Laughing at thinking he could actually do it when he finds out it's already been done. This is a Pharisee hugging a tax collector and kissing a sinner, crying over the unbelievable joy of belonging to such a group—claiming as friends these people he once despised and finding out that he actually *likes* them. This is a Pharisee knowing his old Pharisee friends are probably looking on and judging him as a fool gone off the deep end and not caring one iota what they think.

This is a Pharisee lifting the hem of his robe and dancing.

## Jesus saves

Astonishment is the permanent possession of a forgiven sinner. For our own sake and for the sake of the gospel, we can never become nonchalant about our salvation. Anything more casual and we will give the impression that we actually deserve this status with God. There can be no doubt about how we got here. We have been saved; we have been rescued. We were down to our last breath when God reached out his hand. Anything more than this is arrogance.

Over time, evangelical words like "saved" and "unsaved" can take on a kind of spiritual status that defies their original meaning. We are "saved," and everyone else is "unsaved"—as if to mean we are "in," they are "out." And yet "saved" means just that: plucked from disaster, pulled from the flames, pushed out of the line of fire. Someone else shielded us and took the bullet. We have been saved and we do not know why. Why me and not the other guy? There is absolutely no reason for this. Like a tornado that passed through my town and took my neighbors' houses but left mine standing, there is nothing in me that would indicate I was more worthy than anyone else and that is why my house was spared. In fact, I don't need to know whether my neighbor's loss was some kind of judgment—I am only amazed and grateful for my escape.

*Pharisees* think they deserve their place in the spiritual hierarchy. *Recovering Pharisees* can't believe they even get a place at all. They don't want anyone to check the records too closely for fear a mistake has been made. Instead of *God, I thank you that I am not like that sinner over there*, a recovering Pharisee is more likely thinking, *Why me, Lord? What did I do to merit this kindness? Why me and not him?*

When you really get this, you have to laugh. It's what Frederick Buechner calls the comedy of the gospel. Paul actually seems to be telling a joke when he compares God's presence in our lives to a treasure in a jar. He says we have the treasure of the light and life of Christ taking up residence in our bodies, which, according to him, is nothing to write home about. "But we have this treasure in jars of clay to show that this all-surpassing power is from God and not from us" (2 Corinthians 4:7).

The brilliant light of Christ in a clay pot. This discrepancy is the reason for the whole arrangement in the first place. The incongruity of the vessel and the treasure is designed to make a statement—to actually be something of a joke, so that the obvious contradiction between the two will alleviate any confusion over what went on in our lives. We didn't pull ourselves together. We didn't follow some prescribed path to righteousness for which we can take any credit. We were granted mercy. For all practical purposes this shouldn't be happening. Treasures are never put in such common containers.

Like Ming vases, impressive vessels such as the Pharisees, in their long robes and long, holy faces, draw attention to themselves. Jars of clay, even broken ones, are nothing special. They usually draw attention to what's *in* them. Their usefulness is in what they carry. In Paul's day these vessels were a dime a dozen. Even the poorest family in Jerusalem had an ample supply of clay pots. There is nothing in us that would indicate why God would choose us over any other vessel. We can only be as amazed as anyone.

## Amazing grace

The astonishment of the undeserving believer is not anything new. It was an emotion captured over and over again by many of the early hymn writers.

Consider the following: "And can it be that *I* should gain an interest in my Savior's blood? . . . Amazing love, how can it be, that thou my God should'st die for *me*?" (all emphases mine). Or, "I stand amazed in the presence of Jesus the Nazarene, and wonder how he could love me, a sinner condemned, unclean." And then there is the even more well-known: "Amazing grace, how sweet the sound; that saved a wretch like me. . . ." Or, "I am so glad that Jesus loves me. . . . Jesus loves *even* me." Everywhere you turn in a hymnal it seems you find the shame of sin and the wonder of salvation. "What can wash away my sin? Nothing but the blood of Jesus. . . . Oh, precious is the flow, that makes me white as snow. No other fount I know. Nothing but the blood of Jesus."

In other words, the hymn writers were continually astonished at their salvation. They used words like "marvelous," "wonderful," "matchless," "amazing," and "precious" until they literally ran out of words, and then they simply said, "How shall my tongue describe it? Where shall his praise begin?" And always it is a grace that is greater than our sin. Not just grace, but grace in relationship to the sin in our lives.

The hymnists imagined carrying this expression beyond this earth and right on into heaven: "If there is only one song I can sing, when in

His glory I see the great King; This shall my song in eternity be: Oh, what a wonder that Jesus loves me." They believed that in heaven, the astonishment would continue: "How wonderful! How marvelous, and my song *shall ever be*. How wonderful, how marvelous, is my Savior's love for me." Clearly, these writers were not expecting to be treated this way by God, and they never wanted to forget that fact.

## Surprised by joy!

Astonishment comes from being surprised. It comes from the unexpected. God can surprise publicans, but Pharisees are simply "unsurprisable." God can lift up the poor publican and set him on his feet and give him anything he wants, and he will be baffled by it all. C. S. Lewis called it *Surprised by Joy*, the title of the book chronicling his own conversion. We're surprised because we are getting something we weren't counting on and something we know we don't deserve. We were expecting the worst, and rightfully so, but not only are we not receiving it, we are receiving something beyond our wildest dreams.

Unfortunately, those who are counting on their own righteousness are missing out on the surprise. Usually these people are hedging their bets on a ticket to heaven, but not facing any real depravity in their own soul. If anything, their surprise will come in not having their works accepted.

Our degree of astonishment is related to our personal knowledge of sin. If I have not faced and am not facing the sin in my life, I am not likely to be very impressed with my salvation. It's a nice thing for God to do this for me and all, but I don't really get it. The Pharisees were so far removed from their sin that salvation would have little effect or meaning. Tell a Pharisee that Christ died for him and he will think, *He what? What did he do that for?*

Our worship in the form of astonishment is full of amazement both over who God is and over why, given who he is, he would be interested in being associated with us at all. To stand in his presence and not be struck blind like Saul is pretty remarkable. The Pharisees prided themselves on how much they knew about God, but had they ever had a real encounter with him, they would have been on their knees like the publican.

It's the astonishment of the vagabonds and street people who were ushered into the lavish wedding banquet at the last minute because the invited guests had better things to do. It's the astonishment of the workers who got paid a full day's wage for an hour of work. It's the astonishment of the Prodigal Son welcomed home with a robe, a ring, and a party when all he hoped for was to simply eat with the servants. It's the astonishment of Sarah, who laughed a real laugh, no longer cynical, as the baby Isaac was placed in her old wrinkled arms, chalky white and screaming from birth. It's the thing that will cause all of us to proclaim, when we reach our final destination and first lay eyes on the glories of heaven, "What could I possibly have done to deserve this?"

*Step 1* We admit that our single most unmitigated pleasure is to judge other people.

*Step 2* Have come to believe that our means of obtaining greatness is to make everyone lower than ourselves in our own mind.

*Step 3* Realize that we detest mercy being given to those who, unlike us, haven't worked for it and don't deserve it.

*Step 4* Have decided that we don't want to get what we deserve after all, and we don't want anyone else to either.

*Step 5* Will cease all attempts to apply teaching and rebuke to anyone but ourselves.

*Step 6* Are ready to have God remove all these defects of attitude and character.

*Step 7* Embrace the belief that we are, and will always be, experts at sinning.

*Step 8* Are looking closely at the lives of famous men and  women of the Bible who turned out to be ordinary sinners like us.

*Step 9* Are seeking through prayer and meditation to make a conscious effort to consider others better than ourselves.

*Step 10* Embrace the state of astonishment as a permanent and glorious reality.

*Step 11* Choose to rid ourselves of any attitude that is not bathed in gratitude.

*Step 12* Having had a spiritual awakening as the result of these steps, we will try to carry this message to others who think that Christians are better than everyone else.

# We choose to rid ourselves of any attitude that is not bathed in gratitude.

> The worst moment for an atheist
> comes when he is really thankful and
> has no one to thank.
>
> UNKNOWN

ON THE MOUNTAIN OF HOLINESS THERE IS A WATERSHED FROM which flow two great rivers, the river of Law and the river of Grace. Though they may be joined at the source, the farther they travel on their journeys, the farther apart they become. Just as Moses came down the mountain to find his people engulfed in idolatry and pride, so we can end up far from that which we went to the mountain to seek. It depends entirely upon the course taken. Pharisees always take the river of Law; recovering Pharisees know not to go anywhere but by Grace.

Those who follow the river of Law, though they begin with such high and holy standards, soon find themselves mired in the shallow waters of Deceitfulness and Delusion as they try to maintain an image of themselves that they know in their hearts is not true. Unwilling to admit their own faults and afraid of losing their high position, they choose to continue blindly on until, driven by the current of Hypocrisy, the river empties into the Desert of Burn-out, spent by all the tributaries that depleted its strength on the way down the mountain of Holiness.

The river of Grace, on the other hand, begins with small expectations and gathers strength as it flows. Smaller tributaries continually feed into it until it becomes a wide body of water overflowing its banks on the way to the Sea of Everlasting Life, and the force that moves it along is always Thankfulness. Gratitude is the current of the river of Grace.

The giving of thanks is the only logical response one can have to a forgiveness and a holiness that are totally undeserved. By nature of the fact that grace is a gift, there is nothing one can do but receive it and be thankful for it. Thankfulness is so tied to grace that the absence of gratitude in a Christian's life is an indication that legalism still rules the day.

Pharisees don't respond well to gifts. Gifts are contrary to the pharisaical spirit, which trusts only in what has been earned. Gifts imply a need or a weakness, and if the thing one receives is righteousness, it means admitting to the failure of the holy effort to produce it. The receiver must now become vulnerable to the Giver. But vulnerability is simply not on the Pharisee's list of top ten desirable characteristics. Nor is it very welcome news for Pharisees to find out someone else receives as a free gift what they have been diligently working years to obtain. It's a tragic paradox that Pharisees could have the righteousness they seek, as freely given to them as to anyone, and yet they can never accept it as long as they choose to remain a Pharisee. So the Pharisee is doomed to live a rigid, joyless, and unbending life, lacking in compassion and true human kindness. According to Jesus, their riverbed dried up long ago.

On the other hand, recovering Pharisees like you and me, who have managed to join the ranks of sinners saved by grace, can be found to possess a deep and abiding, ever-flowing gratitude of the heart. We have done nothing to deserve, create, or maintain the righteousness we have been given, and therefore we can do nothing but be grateful for it. Even our reward at the end of the journey will come as a thankful surprise, because we will have become so well acquainted with our sins and shortcomings along the way that we will not be expecting it. So we will throw ourselves on the mercy of God when we meet him, just as we always have done, because we have no other option, and yet, in his eyes, we are already clean. We have been clean all along through the blood of his Son. That's why it will take heaven to contain our praise and an eternity to give proper thanks. "You turned my wailing into dancing; you removed my sackcloth and clothed me with joy, that my heart may sing to you and not be silent. O Lord my God, *I will give you thanks forever*" (Psalm 30:11–12, emphasis mine).

## The mark of gratitude

Since the giving of thanks is the natural result of grace, its presence or lack of presence is an indicator of the basis by which a person lives life. A thankful person will be someone who is daily experiencing at least something of the grace of God, while someone who is bound to the law will be rigid and ungrateful. For Pharisees who have earned their own righteous standing, there is no one to thank—no one, of course, but themselves. So they pray to themselves and thank themselves that they are not like other people who are begging for God's mercy. But all along, those very people who are begging for God's mercy are receiving it and going home justified with hearts full of gratitude. And the Pharisee is thankful that he is not like them? Pity. If only he could be. He would be free of his pride and free of himself. He, too, could go home justified with a thankful heart.

One is thankful only for that which one does not deserve. You don't thank your employer for a paycheck—you earned it—but if your employer decided to give you a Christmas bonus, thanks would be in order. A waitress who receives a 15 percent tip is content with that. She is not overly grateful because 15 percent is what has come to be expected in this business—in effect, it's payment for her hard work. Indeed, she would be a little put out to find only 10 percent there or worse—nothing at all. But imagine her surprise over a table full of middle managers whose CEO threw a crisp one-hundred-dollar bill down on top of a 20 percent credit card tip, out of simple generosity or a show of wealth. There would be a lot of rejoicing back in the kitchen, especially if the waitress decided to share her good fortune with the rest of the staff.

Pharisees are always dealing in the realm of paychecks and proper remuneration for services rendered. Recovering Pharisees are always dealing in bonuses, surprises, and the unexpected. Everything that is good in life is seen as a bonus. They walk around grateful for every breath, every sunset, every new morning, every color in the color spectrum, and every star in the sky. Like an alcoholic who is clean and sober, noticing beauty and taste for the first time, recovering Pharisees are grateful just to be alive because they have been dead for so long.

## The overcoming power of a thankful heart

Like a steady flowing river that irrigates its surroundings, the benefits of a thankful heart are many. It's hard to think of one vice that the virtue of thankfulness cannot render useless. One does not need to steal when one is thankful. Since when has a person filled with gratitude stolen anything? A man does not covet his neighbor's wife when he is thankful for his own. A single person does not harbor jealousy toward married people when she has discovered how to be thankful for her singleness. No one craves more when he is grateful for what he has.

In like manner, envy and pride are the enemies of thankfulness. "For where you have envy and selfish ambition, there you find disorder and every evil practice" (James 3:16). To which could be added, where you have a heart ruled by gratitude you will find neither envy nor selfish ambition. Thankfulness conquers selfish ambition. "I have learned to be content whatever the circumstances," said Paul (Philippians 4:11).

For this reason, giving thanks is one of the most valuable tools a recovering Pharisee has in fighting pharisaical attitudes. A thankful heart cancels out many if not all the flaws of a Pharisee. There isn't one pharisaical characteristic Jesus spoke out against that is not stripped of its power by a thankful heart. No need to judge other people when you are thankful for who you are. No need to measure yourself by and compare yourself to others when you are thankful for what God has done in your life. No need to stand at the door of the kingdom of God and keep others out when you're just thankful that you got in. God can let in anyone he wants. It's up to him. You are simply glad to be counted among the saved.

You don't care if you get the important seat at the table when you are overcome with gratitude at simply being invited to the dinner. You don't put heavy weights on other people's shoulders when you are thankful that God has lightened your own load. You are not obsessed with what other people think of you when you are overwhelmed with the fact that God is thinking about you all the time. You don't demand respect when you are thankful for your place. You don't have to hide your own sin when you have received God's forgiveness. You don't have to maintain an outward show when God has cleaned up your heart. You don't have to protect your image when you are already number one with God. You don't have to condemn other people's blindness when it's only the grace of God that has allowed you to see. You don't have to try for the highest place when you are already grateful for the lowest. You don't have to make a show of spirituality when you are thankful for having received the Spirit. You don't have to clothe yourself in holy robes when you already have been clothed in righteousness. You don't have to be full of yourself when you are thankful that God has filled you up with himself.

## Antidote to pride

Since gratitude is such a powerful tool in eradicating pharisaical judgments and attitudes, it is good periodically to take inventory of our lives and check for things like resentment, pride, envy, and judgment. Once identified, we can apply thanksgiving to the situation and watch what happens. Here's an example of what I mean.

There is a certain young man whose book has sold, at this writing, over six hundred thousand units in the Christian market. It is a book about aspects of the single life covered in a similar way in a message I gave over twenty-five years ago when I was single. The church I was attending at the time printed my talk, and its circulation over the years has been almost as wide as this new book. However, because it was a pamphlet, not a book, and it was provided largely at cost to anyone who requested it, I never received any proceeds from this rather large demand. That was fine for quite some time—this was ministry in my mind, and God used it in surprising ways. I had nothing to do with it— no marketing, no promotion. My church's printing ministry merely responded to requests that flooded in from all over the world. That was the way I wanted it . . . up until now.

Now suddenly I am filled with regret that I never turned that pamphlet into a book (I've thought of it more than a few times). I notice in me a growing anger over the fact that someone else did, and took it to the bank in the form of a highly successful venture. I am even aware of being angry with God for not letting this happen to me. I start to imagine what I could do if I ever sold six hundred thousand copies of anything. I could erase some debts, pay for my son's and daughter's college education, secure a nice retirement fund for my wife, and take a long overdue vacation. Instead, some twenty-something guy who doesn't even have a family to support is sitting on a gold mine for something I thought of twenty-five years ago.

You don't want to go with me too much further down this road; believe me, it's not a very pretty sight. It is a road that runs through envy and selfish ambition, the very things that James said were responsible for "disorder and every evil practice," which would include, of course, the resentment and bitterness that follows.

So what do I do about this? How does this recovering Pharisee recover from a lapse into judging a young man who simply found what he found and did something about it? The answer is found in giving thanks. I start by being thankful that the message has gone out and has helped so many people. I remember that I—as well as this other gentleman—am only the messenger; it's the message that's important, and however that message goes forth, I will rejoice in it. I will remember that I may have planted the seed, and someone else may have watered it, but God made it grow (1 Corinthians 3:6). I will also be mindful of the fact that God will supply all my needs according to his riches in Christ Jesus, and I can trust him in this and thank him in advance. And I can get down on my knees and confess my envy and selfish ambition and plead for God's mercy and then be thankful when I get it. There is simply no way to be thankful and resentful at the same time. Either one rules.

Perhaps now would be a good time to put this book down and apply this step to something in your own life over which you are harboring pride or resentment or hardheadedness. I guarantee that giving heartfelt, genuine thanks will begin to change everything.

## The great divorce

What we are talking about is a resignation of any claim to credit for what is good in our lives and putting in its place a thankfulness to God, the Giver of the very things we are giving up. I am reminded in this regard of *The Great Divorce* by C. S. Lewis, where an imaginary busload of folks from hell get to take a trip to the outskirts of heaven and check it out for a while. The implication is that they may get to relocate should they so choose—a sort of eternal second chance.

In the process, these spirits from hell meet people they knew in life from their various disciplines—an artist from hell meets an artist from heaven, an intellectual meets a fellow intellectual, a professor meets another professor from the same university, and so forth. In every case, as they talk, it becomes evident that the residents of hell are reluctant to part with what the residents of heaven abandoned long before they got there. The artist from hell, for instance, can't give up the urge to paint everything and not simply experience it. (In heaven there is no need to paint, because they are enjoying that which they were trying to paint all along on earth. They were trying to grasp for perfection; in heaven they have the thing itself.) The intellectual can't give up his own slant on truth and accept the Truth. The professor can't live with no one to teach, and here everyone knows everything there is to know.

In stark contrast, their heaven-bound counterparts have let go of what they now regard as small things, be it their pride, or their ownership of their work, or their control over their image, and have received so much more in return, for which they are eternally grateful. At one point in the story, an artist from heaven shows an artist from hell a fountain, which, upon drinking its waters, cleanses a person of the need to be attached to their own works—a thought that utterly horrifies the artist from hell.

It becomes more and more obvious as this visit continues that the residents from hell are still carrying their anger, their bitterness, and their pride with a grip that has so calcified their fingers they cannot let go. And so, satisfied that heaven is not the place for them, these wandering spirits reboard their bus and head back to hell by their own choice, for in the chilling wisdom of Lewis's observation, they wanted it this way all along.

## No different than a sinner

Returning to the parable of the Pharisee and the tax collector, it seems the Pharisee can drum up only one kind of thankfulness—that being to thank himself that he is not like the tax collector. He fasts, he tithes, and he has measurable proof that he is "better." It should come as no surprise then, that a similar prayer for a recovering Pharisee would begin with a complete reversal of this attitude.

*Dear God, I am thankful that, when all is said and done, I am no different than that sinner over there. I need you more than anybody. These robes are getting heavy and this show is getting old and burdensome. Have mercy on me, Lord, not only because I am a sinner but because I have thought and acted for so long as if I were not. I have hidden myself behind the illusion of being good, and I am ready to be stripped of all my self-righteousness and selfish pride. Make room for me next to the tax collector over there, and if you still have a place in your kingdom, just getting in the door would be good enough for me.*

*Step 1* We admit that our single most unmitigated pleasure is to judge other people.

*Step 2* Have come to believe that our means of obtaining greatness is to make everyone lower than ourselves in our own mind.

*Step 3* Realize that we detest mercy being given to those who, unlike us, haven't worked for it and don't deserve it.

*Step 4* Have decided that we don't want to get what we deserve after all, and we don't want anyone else to either.

*Step 5* Will cease all attempts to apply teaching and rebuke to anyone but ourselves.

*Step 6* Are ready to have God remove all these defects of attitude and character.

*Step 7* Embrace the belief that we are, and will always be, experts at sinning.

*Step 8* Are looking closely at the lives of famous men and women of the Bible who turned out to be ordinary sinners like us.

*Step 9* Are seeking through prayer and meditation to make a conscious effort to consider others better than ourselves.

*Step 10* Embrace the state of astonishment as a permanent and glorious reality.

*Step 11* Choose to rid ourselves of any attitude that is not bathed in gratitude.

*Step 12* Having had a spiritual awakening as the result of these steps, we will try to carry this message to others who think that Christians are better than everyone else.

*Having had a spiritual awakening as the result of these steps, we will try to carry this message to others who think that Christians are better than everyone else.*

---

ANYONE WHO HAS BEEN A CHRISTIAN FOR ANY LENGTH OF TIME probably knows what it's like to be treated as if you weren't cut out of the same cloth as most ordinary human beings. This is the part of Pharisaism for which Christians may not be entirely to blame. Non-Christians make their own contribution to our pharisaical condition sometimes, if they think they have something to gain by it. And they do. By making Christians appear as distant and odd, they can ensure that no one in their right mind (themselves, mostly) would want to be one.

They can also counter the real guilt pang or moral regret that might surface from being around someone who is genuinely seeking righteousness. Someone whose heart is after God, but "normal" in all other respects, presents a problem to many non-Christians, but someone prudish and self-righteous . . . well, no one wants to be like that. It's a kind of mutual agreement people in the world have to discredit Christians. If deep down you know you are a sinner, but you don't want to admit it or do anything about it, then it's natural to want to take a few potshots at saints.

## "Could it be . . . SATAN?"

Dana Carvey's church lady, popular on the television show *Saturday Night Live* in the late '80s and sure to make a comeback in some form, is a perfect example of how unbelievers like to characterize Christians. And no one makes a better caricature of a modern-day Pharisee than the church lady. Dressed in a heavy gray wool suit and seated in a gold straight-backed chair in front of a stained-glass window, with pointed glasses, hands folded, and pursed lips, the church lady is the perfect expression of what everyone hates about a self-righteous, judgmental person. Her trademark line, "Well, isn't that *spe-shul!*" makes a mockery of personal piety.

The popularity and appeal of the church lady demonstrates that non-Christians have us pegged as Pharisees from the start. Superiority and judgment are common pharisaical themes the church lady relentlessly satirizes. "Well, if I'm not God's favorite, let me explode right now" is a good example, and she would often close her "Church Chat" sketch by doing the "Superior Dance" with a guest. In his Las Vegas show, Carvey's church lady bursts onto the stage and immediately passes judgment on the throngs of beautiful women (and what they are wearing) in the front rows.

Repeated attacks like this on the idea of personal virtue can wear down a person's good conscience and often quell whatever might be right about sincere spiritual urges. But though this satirical ribbing seems to originate in the non-Christian camp, we are not entirely innocent in the matter. Where do these images come from, if not from experiences people have had with real Christians? And even if we are not creating these impressions ourselves, to what extent are we perpetuating them?

## Sitting ducks

The typical non-Christian idea of a Christian is someone who tries to be better. Actually "better" is being generous; "better than . . ." is probably more like it. It's more than ethical morality; it's pharisaical look-down-your-nose-at-everyone-else morality. To a certain extent, this impression is a witnessing strategy gone awry.

Somewhere along the line Christian leaders began to perpetuate the myth that if we lived lives that were better than everyone else's, it would make Christianity attractive to the world. "Be perfect and everyone will want to be like us," or so we thought. Perhaps at one time this actually worked. Maybe a long time ago it was a shared goal of everyone to be a virtuous person. But if it ever was, it isn't today. Cynicism dominates the hero market. Virtue is mocked everywhere. When leaders, beginning with our country's president on down, are shown to have shifty feet and shiftier zippers, any attempt at true character only makes one a target.

A cartoon artist whose work shows in a gallery near my home has a painting of a Donald-Duck-type character lounging in a beach chair with a drink, a good book, and a large bullet hole blasted into the stucco wall behind him only a few inches above his head. The title of the piece is "Sitting Duck." Christians who try to perpetuate squeaky clean images are sitting ducks in a world obsessed with duck hunting, and you can be sure that it will always be open season on our pharisaical practices.

This attack is not necessarily a bad thing; it can help to sharpen our senses, aiding us in discerning what is true Christianity and what is a phony distortion. And it certainly would not be a good idea to fight back. We should probably take it in stride in a good-natured sort of way, as one would take a joke that made fun of something marginal in one's character or personality. A person with a good self-image can handle such a thing. So, in like manner, a Christian who is secure in Christ can take some teasing about pharisaism; after all, we should dislike self-righteousness as much as anybody.

I always liked the church lady. I saw in her the things I don't like about myself and the misleading aspects of a Christianity with which I am all too familiar. I never took her as an attack on my faith; I took her as an attack on everything that is false and hypocritical about Christianity. We really should point and laugh along with the world on this one. The joke is on us, and to a certain extent we deserve it.

## Branding

If the truth were told, none of us is as good as we make ourselves out to be, and though we would all probably agree about this, we aren't exactly getting this point across to the world. We are pragmatists at heart, trying to show that as Christians we are happier, better, and more fulfilled than everybody else. This perpetuation of a high and holy example at any cost—even the cost of honesty—has become our cherished witness in the world and one of our biggest mistakes.

This "witness" has taken on various forms over the years, from excusing oneself from "social dancing" (something I did in my grammar school days) to turning down a drink at an office party and thinking some great victory has just been won for Christ and his kingdom as a result of our unflinching stand.

Actually, as far as drinking and dancing and a host of other things like this go, most non-Christians couldn't care less whether we do or don't. They will make a deal about it only because we make a deal about it, and they like catching us in our own traps. It wouldn't be hypocritical to drink at an office party if we hadn't made it a Christian issue in the first place. What we think is witnessing in this regard is not witnessing at all. It's what the advertising world calls *branding*.

Branding is what identifies a product or a service and sets it apart in an easily recognizable manner. True witnessing is nothing more than telling somebody about Jesus. There is a big difference between these two. One is an image, the other is a message. One is conjured up, the other is simply shared. I think that as Christians we've been better at conserving the image than we have been at conveying the message. We're good at branding ourselves as singular Christians but not at introducing people to Christ. In my experience, asking the person on the street to define a Christian will bear this out. Typical definitions yield very little about Jesus and a lot about issues and attitudes that set us apart from everyone else—definitions that put us squarely in the Pharisee camp.

Some people want to be Christians and would be if it weren't for this "branding" of Christians that obscures the truth.

For instance, a person may have a heart of compassion, a keen interest in the truth, and an intuitive sense that Jesus is right, yet still be thought of as an outsider when it comes to the church. The reason for this often has little to do with one's real spiritual hunger as much as it has to do with one's stand on behavioral and cultural issues. It's sad but true that a person's belonging or lack of belonging to the church today can be related more to political and moral issues than it is to Christ and salvation.

The church exists for people who don't understand it all but who love Jesus, people who are always questioning things because they want to know the truth, and people who know they are sinners in need of a Savior, and yet these are the very people who often find a church a phony place full of Pharisees. Where does a pro-choice Democrat with homosexual struggles go to church today? Not many churches I know of. For that matter, where does a sinner go to church?

The gospel is just what it is: good news for sinners. The only people who should be offended by it are people who can't admit their sin. No one who can admit their sin is an offense to the gospel. Yet Christians today seem to carry a long list of offensive people, not the least of which are homosexuals, pro-choice advocates, rock stars, feminists, sex educators, atheists, Hollywood producers, and the list goes on. And yet no one on this list is an enemy of the gospel ("For our struggle is not against flesh and blood . . ." Ephesians 6:12). No one on this list is out of range of the gospel ("And that is what some of you were. But you were washed, you were sanctified . . ." 1 Corinthians 6:11). *Everyone* on this list is one step away from admitting their sin, just like us. And any sinner who can do that is one confession away from heaven. Sin is the only offense; the brand of sin is inconsequential.

## Blast off!

I carry a brochure around with me that advertises a motivational leadership seminar. I am sure it is similar to the typical supercharged locker room pep talks that characterize many sales conventions and multi-level marketing schemes. I've been to sessions like this before, and they do charge you up for a while. However, in a Christian context (and this particular one was led by a well-known pastor), they merely keep alive the I've-got-it-all-together-you-should-be-like-me myth, and make it even more dangerous by turning it into a model of leadership.

Each page of the colorful, slick brochure pictures a historic form of flight that took you higher, farther, faster. First there's this guy wearing some kind of bird-wing contraption with the caption "You're up to the challenge of leadership. (Potential maximum altitude: 3 feet.)" Next is a picture of something Orville and Wilbur Wright would have flown. Its caption: "You've taken flight as a leader. (Potential maximum altitude: 300 feet.)" Turn the page and there is a 1950s vintage DC–3 way up in the clouds: "You're ready to soar to the next level as a leader. (Potential maximum altitude: 23,000 feet.)" And finally, with the whole thing unfolded in front of you, it's the space shuttle blasting off into the darkness of outer space over the blue-green rim of the world. "Now launch yourself into unlimited potential as a leader. (Potential maximum altitude: Unlimited.)"

I've always looked at that brochure and imagined this leader's followers standing around Cape Kennedy watching that little glowing dot disappear into the endless blue.

"Wow! There he goes."

"Yeah. What a guy! That's our leader."

"Sure is. Boy, are we lucky. What adventures lie ahead for him! Look, he's just a dot now."

"I lost him. I can't see him anymore."

"Think he's ever coming back?"

"Who knows?"

"I wonder what we're supposed to do now?"

I believe this is exactly what happens when we perpetuate this high and holy model of leadership and Christian life. We blast ourselves right off the planet. And we're just too high up to relate to anyone but ourselves.

## Show and tell

*We are not as good as we make ourselves out to be, but we aren't exactly getting that point across to the world.* Well, believe it or not, this is the point we need to be making. Our sins and doubts and mistakes are no threat to our witness: they are an integral part of it. In its simplest form, our greatest witness to the world is to show and tell how much we need Jesus. Yes, the pronoun is right. Though our job may seem to have been to show people how much *they* need Jesus, we now as recovering Pharisees have a new job description: to show people how much *we* need Jesus.

It's almost like a secret. Tell people how much you need the Lord and they will hang around for a while and wonder why. When they find out that you have the same sins and fears and questions that they have, they just might start to wonder if they need the Lord, too. Pretty soon, you're leading someone to the Lord and you've never even told them anything. You've only told them how much you need Jesus in your life.

This secret doesn't only apply to Christians and non-Christians, it applies to Christians and Christians as well. Some pastors major in telling the members of their congregation how much they (the members) need the Lord. What goes along with that is an assumption that the pastor obviously doesn't. That's why he's the pastor. The people are the ones who need the Lord and it's the pastor's job to remind them of that. This is the way a pharisaical pastor would preach.

My pastor, on the other hand, is a recovering Pharisee, so he keeps telling us how much he needs Jesus, and he preaches this way every Sunday. Each week we find out in a new way how much he needs the Lord. It's so refreshing. (I used to wonder why I seem to cry a lot in this church; now I know.) I haven't heard from many recovering Pharisees in my life.

When my pastor tells his own story, somewhere in it I find mine, and the strength God gives him to meet his own needs is somehow made available to me right there on the spot. It's as if he gets it for me—as if he is always one struggle ahead of the rest of us.

## *"It's about your kids. . . ."*

It happened again just this last Sunday. In the course of his message our pastor admitted to a fear of his that happens to be a big one for me too: the nagging vexation that he hasn't done enough for his kids. "I haven't done enough to prepare them and put them on the right path to lead them to God," was exactly what he said.

Fear gripped my heart. He had just voiced one of my greatest concerns. What was he going to say now? So I was all ears when he said he remembers in these times that there is only one reason he is in Christ. It is only the kindness of God. He is not in Christ because his father was a pastor and he came from a Christian family. Plenty of kids have grown up in similar circumstances and have gone in other directions. The only explanation for his own relationship with God is God's kindness. It is the answer of God's mercy and God's mercy alone.

As my wife and I walked out of church that day we were met by a woman on a mission. I was overwhelmed because she came right up to me and started talking to me about this very issue as if she had been reading my mind.

"I know how you feel about your kids and I have something for you." I looked around to make sure she was talking to me. How did she know that part of the sermon hit me hard? Was this a prophecy? An angel? A messenger from God?

"Just remember," she burst in on my thoughts of amazement, "if your kids were perfect they wouldn't need Jesus."

It was then that I realized she thought I was the pastor. We both have the same landing strip on top of our heads. She was comforting him and comforting me instead. I joked with him later that I, like Jacob, had stolen his blessing. It occurs to me that it's a good church whose pastor the people can comfort. That's the church of the recovering Pharisee.

It also occurs to me that the woman's statement goes further than just my kids, your kids, my pastor's kids. It goes for us all. If we were perfect we wouldn't need Jesus. If there were a slogan for a recovering Pharisee (and I'm not recommending it because I hate slogans), it would be this: "If we were perfect we wouldn't need Jesus."

Pharisees don't need Jesus. They have blasted off into the stratosphere never to be seen again, because they are off leading seminars on how to blast off. Recovering Pharisees need Jesus, and that is their message. And usually they can be found struggling along with the rest of us.

## Fault line

What's happening here is truly wonderful. We are now coming to see our imperfections as being not only a part of the message, but useful to it. If our witness is to show people how much we need Jesus, then our witness will of necessity have in it the components of our failures, our worries, our inadequacies, our mistakes, and our sins. If we didn't have these things, we wouldn't need Jesus. In short, all the things Pharisees try to hide are right out in the open for recovering Pharisees. Without them we would have no witness.

There also is an unfortunate reversal of this equation. "Perfect" people have no witness. They have nothing to give anyone. You can give only what you have received, and Pharisees, unfortunately for their followers, have earned everything. Likewise, all those perfect Christians running around being great examples for Christ have no witness at all. They are, in fact, doing grave damage to the gospel. They are perpetuating the myth that Christians are better than anybody else and driving away those who truly need the good news of salvation through Jesus Christ.

I'm not saying by this that Christians are not good people. Jesus talks about bringing honor to God by our good deeds, and Peter talks about having good reputations among the people of the world. But when anyone gets close to us, they should discover our secret. We are just like anyone else, but for Christ. We've got to tell them this because if we don't, they may get focused on us and not Christ. I actually think a lot of Christians try to model Christ devoid of his compassion. They have themselves roped off in some spiritual VIP section away from the company of average sinners. This is a shame because it is not necessary.

We can sidle up to non-Christians and they can sidle up to us because we have a lot in common. We can show them that their sin is no barrier to God anymore because Jesus has paid the price for it. And in observing our daily need for Christ and his power and forgiveness, they hopefully will find their own need for him.

## The real story

Many Christians believe the real work of facing sin and forgiveness is something to be done in private so that we can present to the world not the process but the finished product. Like bodybuilders who flex their muscles and grease themselves down for show, we pump up our spirituality as much as possible for display to the world, when all along the world probably would just as likely respond to an average guy with a beer belly and a forgiven heart.

Truth of the matter is, we don't need all this spiritual stuff we put on; we only need a Savior. And we have one! The world doesn't get a different message than we get. The world gets the same message; we are all sinners in need of a Savior. We don't tell them only part of the story and leave the rest for later. We tell it all up front and then we keep living it and illustrating it with our own living and depending on Christ. We will have more opportunities to share our faith as honest, forgiven sinners than we ever will have as drop-dead holy saints.

And what's so difficult about this anyway? You don't need to go to training to learn how to be a forgiven sinner; you just tell your story. It's not that hard. We don't need the four laws, or the five steps, or the ten basic elements of Christian witnessing, we just need a real story—our story—and if we don't have one, we should pay attention to God in our lives until we do.

The same things that will keep us from being pharisaical (humility, weakness, vulnerability, honesty) will make us better witnesses in the world. It's all in God's wacky economy. Less is more. Lower is higher. Worse is better. Weaker is stronger. Showing the world our worst is going to do more for the gospel than showing the world our best. And because non-Christians have us pegged as the church lady, we may have to go out of our way to be human in order to get this across. The world doesn't help us out in this way at all. The world would rather have us being holy than have us being real. The church lady is easier to dismiss than someone who is honestly facing his or her faults. Faults make us real. Faults make us human.

## In the company of sinners

Here is a simple saying recovering Pharisees need to remember: *Being saved is better than being better.* Being saved will get the true essence of the gospel across much better than being better or being happy or being holy or being perfect. Somehow, we've got to get the spotlight off pharisaical self-righteousness and back on the gospel. The gospel is, and will always be, the point; and the gospel is all about being saved. Being better puts us in with the Pharisees; being saved puts us in the company of sinners.

There is a short story by the remarkable southern writer Flannery O'Connor called "Revelation" that ends with a vision of this. It was published in *The Sewanee Review* in the spring of 1964, just a few months before the author's death. The story is about a woman named Mrs. Turpin, sitting in a doctor's crowded waiting room with her husband, who had been kicked by a horse. Though on the surface she is cordial and kind to everyone, underneath she passes judgment on "niggers, white trashy people," and all the other lowlifes in the room. She prides herself in the fact that she has always lived a virtuous, proper life "with common sense and respectable behavior." Basically, she is disdainful of everyone who is not as "proper" as she.

Mrs. Turpin's quiet condemnation fails to escape the notice of an overweight, acne-faced, "white trashy" girl whose simmering anger over Mrs. Turpin's snide innuendoes finally overcomes her. Flying out of control, the girl throws her book at the woman and tries to strangle her. A nurse in the office subdues her, but not before she whispers to Mrs. Turpin, "Go back to hell where you belong, you old warthog."

At home on her farm, Mrs. Turpin confronts God. Was this experience a message from him? She demands of God, "Who do you think you are?" And standing at the pen that contains her prize pigs, with the sun setting, she receives a vision. Flannery O'Connor describes what she saw:

> Until the sun slipped finally behind the tree line, Mrs. Turpin remained there with her gaze bent to them [her prize, super-sanitized pigs] as if she were absorbing some abysmal life-giving knowledge. At last she lifted her head. There was only a purple streak in the sky, cutting through a field of crimson and leading, like an extension of the highway, into the descending dusk. She raised her hands from the side of the pen in a gesture hieratic and profound. A visionary light settled in her eyes. She saw the streak as a vast swinging bridge extending upward from the earth through a field of living fire. Upon it a vast horde of souls were rumbling toward heaven. There were whole companies of white-trash, clean for the first time in their lives, and bands of black niggers in white robes, and battalions of freaks and lunatics shouting and clapping and leaping like frogs. And bringing up the end of the procession was a tribe of people whom she recognized at once as those who, like herself and Claud [her husband], had always had a little of everything and the God-given wit to use it right. She leaned forward to observe them closer. They were marching behind the others with great dignity, accountable as they had always been for good order and common sense and respectable behavior. Yet she could see by their shocked and altered faces that even their virtues were being burned away.

The final verse of "The Only One" (John Fischer), quoted in chapter 5:

> *And then I saw as in a dream*
> *Reflections of His glory stream*
> *On unsuspecting faces*
> *Enraptured in His graces.*
> *And the lost who now had all been found*
> *Sang in pure unfettered sound*
> *A song I knew from memory*

*Though I'd never heard it sung before.*
*And then the host brought out the wine*
*And bid us all come and dine*
*At the banquet of the living—*
*The table of forgiving.*
*And as we raised our glasses high*
*And tears were forming in our eyes*
*I heard His words remind me*
*Of what I'd heard so many times before.*
*You're not the only one with truth,*
*You're not the only one with eyes,*
*You're not the only one—the only one who cries.*
*You're not the only one.*

May God burn away our "virtues" if they keep us from the company of those, including ourselves, whom he came to save.

# Study Questions

## Step 1

1. Why is it that we tend to develop a strong, established "out-look" on life but neglect to foster a truthful, searching "in-look"?
2. How does an inwardly judgmental attitude gradually shift our standard from being focused on God to being focused on people? What are the dangers of comparing ourselves to others?
3. By setting our own "standard," in what way(s) is our view of reality altered? How can spiritual arrogance bring us to the point of assuming that our standard has become God's standard?
4. Can you think of anyone you would not want to be with in heaven? Give your reasons.
5. Judging others used to be pleasurable for us. Now, knowing that we will be measured according to the measure we use, why does it make sense to be a "recovering Pharisee"?

## Step 2

1. Why do we frequently have one scale of mercy for ourselves and another for those around us? Why do we feel we deserve mercy while we judge others harshly?
2. In what ways do you find yourself putting others down in order to elevate yourself? Is your action implicit or explicit? Mental or verbal?

3. What kind of accountability could you implement to more quickly recognize and address your inclination to put others below yourself?

4. Who serves as a two-way mirror in your life? Does this person or persons have the freedom to be honest with you? Do you seek the truth about yourself as they see it?

5. Do your friends protect you and one another from vulnerability, or are they committed to the truth? Can you think of "no-talk" rules that exist within your circles? Why are certain things off limits?

6. What are some questions that could be asked among your friends that would keep everyone honest?

## Step 3

1. Why is it unreasonable to be indignant when others receive something they don't deserve? Or when they don't receive what they do deserve?

2. What keeps us from recognizing that there is nothing we can do to earn our standing with God?

3. From a pharisaical standpoint, why is trying to live out the law "easier" than living by grace? How does this relate to fallen humanity's tendency to live in isolation rather than in intimacy?

4. How can our preoccupation with measuring what others deserve be a constant reminder to us that we ought to prefer God's grace to seeking our own reward? What if we got what we have earned?

5. What kind of people do you consider to be "undesirable"? How would you react to their sin being pardoned?

6. Are there things in your life that you have added to the law that you take pride in keeping? What are they? Have you in any way redefined "sin" to fit your own desires and perspectives?

7. How can worship weaken the vise of our control? How can acknowledging God for who he is bring us into the enjoyment of his grace?

## Step 4

1. In what way can a parent showing mercy to a child be more effective than by showing justice? Who are the child's primary reflectors of God's nature and character?
2. What is your natural response to "common grace"? Why do Christians in general have a hard time accepting that non-Christians enjoy good things?
3. This is the day of salvation. What does that change for us? What perspectives, attitudes, and goals are affected as we seek to be vessels of God's grace?
4. If we are going to be the light of Christ to this world today, what is our calling according to Romans 2:1–5; 2 Corinthians 6:2; and 2 Peter 3:9, 15?
5. How does not showing mercy to others reveal that we are not leaning on God's mercy for our own salvation?
6. Who are your "enemies"? Is it more common for you to think of and pray for their salvation or their judgment?

## Step 5

1. How do you feel about not being in a position to teach others? What do you learn from your feelings in this area?
2. How can we know the difference between being angry at something because it is sinful and being angry because of sin in our own lives? When is anger justifiable? What does our anger tell us?
3. What parts of the gospel of Jesus Christ are we suppressing or denying in order to maintain our position, status, or platform?
4. Are we losing our childlike wonder? Is there a reason others are afraid to tell us we are becoming hardened and critical?
5. What can we learn from Jesus' response to Nicodemus? How is it possible to know the truth and yet not be born again? How can we have the answer and still be avoiding the question?

## Step 6

1. Why is ethical/legalistic righteousness irrelevant? Why can't we be saved on technicalities? Why is it never enough?
2. Does the beginning of your story as a recovering Pharisee bear any similarity to Paul's? Were you in a sense knocked from your horse or blinded by Christ's brilliance? What factors and experiences have made you aware of your need for grace?
3. In what ways do you feel you are being humbled as you journey along God's way? What blind spots have you discovered?
4. Once we have an awareness of sin, what are our options? Why is "middle ground" impossible once we realize what we really are apart from the sacrifice of Jesus?
5. Is there anyone in your life whom you once considered inferior but whom you have had to learn to trust in order to experience God's freedom? Is there anyone whom you still believe is beneath you in any way?
6. Do you still have any investments in "pseudo-spiritual bank accounts" that need to be liquidated? Do you have any self-achieved assets that have not yet been tossed on the refuse pile?

## Step 7

1. Why is it so damaging to both leaders and followers alike to live in an atmosphere of denial? Why do we wish to live in a structured and ranked hierarchy rather than in a community of fellowship and equality?
2. What are the inevitable messages we send to our struggling fellow believers and also to non-Christians when we claim we are completely victorious over sin?
3. If we are relying on ourselves to "get us through," have we experienced God's grace? Is it possible to truly encounter God's grace but choose to reject it or to supplement it with human effort? What can we learn from the Galatians about the deception of works-righteousness?

4. Is the experience of confession and forgiveness as fresh in your life as it was at your conversion? If not, do you believe it can be?

5. Does the discovery of more sin in our lives mean we are regressing? How can intimacy with God and fellowship with others be compatible with a constant and growing awareness of sin?

## Step 8

1. In what ways was your early Bible education/Sunday school experience similar to that described in this chapter? How did you feel when you found out the truth about the biblical characters?

2. Are there any human figures in the Bible whose sin it seems should disqualify them from the place they were given? Why? What is your reaction to the sin of that person or those people? Does he or she resemble you in any way?

3. Has anything in your life led you to think that God cannot use you? If so, why? Is anything too sinful or too ugly or too shameful to be used by God for his glory?

4. If God gets more glory working through sinful people than "righteous" ones, why shouldn't we aim to sin, knowing that his grace will be all the more visible in the light of our failure? What does Paul mean when he addresses this in Romans 6?

5. Taking the teaching of this eighth chapter of *12 Steps* as a model, what changes do we need to be considering and enacting in the local church?

## Step 9

1. Do we have a responsibility to consider criticism even if it is delivered in a way that is not constructive? Is there anyone from whom we should not accept criticism?

2. How can we consider others better than ourselves without having a self-image problem? If we consider ourselves to be the least of the least, how can we believe that we have value?

3. If everyone else's sin is none of our business, how are we accountable

to each other? Is there any place for confrontation in our Christian walk? What are the guiding principles for this issue?

4. How would seeing with the eyes of Jesus instead of our own make a difference in our relationships?

5. How is it possible that there is something true or noble or right or pure or lovely or admirable in *every* person? Is there anyone you can think of for whom this is not the case? Even through Christ's eyes?

## Step 10

1. Have you ever taken a particular virtue, isolated it, and done everything in your power to perfect it? What was the result? If you haven't done this, do you think it's possible?

2. In your experience, does the local church reflect the opening statements of Jesus in the Sermon on the Mount? Why or why not?

3. If our salvation, or our being chosen by God, doesn't amaze us, what are we missing? To whom is salvation truly the greatest gift? Is it possible to be "good" enough that the wonder of salvation is diminished in our lives?

4. Are confession and repentance a natural part of your church experience?

5. Have you ever seen a Pharisee dance? Can you picture it?

## Step 11

1. At what point in your spiritual journey did you begin to realize it was pharisaism that was depleting your life of joy and gratitude? What factors or situations heightened the awareness of your heart's condition?

2. Other than for specific occasions, such as your birthday, is it difficult for you to expect something you feel you haven't earned? Do you know why?

3. What kind of poverty can overtake a thankful heart? Could you ever have so little that you would have nothing to offer someone else? At

what point is complaining justified?

4. Is there anything for which you are not thankful? Is there anything you assume is your right and can therefore be taken for granted? Why?

## Step 12

1. What is your initial response to being made sport of by the world for being a believer? Is the ridicule simply because you are a Christian, or because you are a Pharisee? Would the criticism be different in each case?

2. Why does knowing who we are in Christ become so important when facing the mocking of the world? How can we respond in the way Jesus would?

3. Write out a quick list: What examples of "branding" can you see if you take an honest look at your life? In what ways have you focused more on an image than on a message?

4. How can an abortion doctor or a pornographer be closer to God's kingdom than a church member or a church officer?

5. How does being vulnerable about struggles enhance rather than harm our witness? Are there certain things we should keep under wraps? Are there any lines that need to be drawn? Why?

*Thank you for selecting a book from*
BETHANY HOUSE PUBLISHERS

Bethany House Publishers is a ministry of Bethany Fellowship International, an interdenominational, nonprofit organization committed to spreading the Good News of Jesus Christ around the world through evangelism, church planting, literature distribution, and care for those in need. Missionary training is offered through Bethany College of Missions.

Bethany Fellowship International is a member of the National Association of Evangelicals and subscribes to its statement of faith. If you would like further information, please contact:

Bethany Fellowship International
6820 Auto Club Road
Minneapolis, MN 55438 USA